READY, SET, WAIT.

The Unadulterated Truth about Navigating
Sex, Singleness, and Abstinence
as a Christian Woman

Sade Solomon

Published by Solomon Creative, LLC

Printed in the United States of America

ISBN 979-8-9863973-0-6

Cover design by Solomon Creative, LLC

This book is dedicated
to my father, William Solomon,
who showed me what a man's love should feel like.

To my mother, Cheryl Reese,
whose humility and love gave me the space to heal.

To single women
who feel overlooked, undesirable, and forgotten,
know that I love you and God does too.

Table of Contents

Why I Wrote This Book?

I bet you've all been there!

You're scrolling through Instagram minding your business...

Then BAM... you're hit in the gut by a post by another relationship "expert." The post explains the five steps single Black women can take to find love. The thing is, you are familiar with the message, it is the same message you see from every Instagram relationship "expert" on the interweb.

It is a message aimed at single Black women, and a journey we are called to embark on. A journey that leads to us being less independent, weaker, more docile, quieter, less accomplished, a little more modest about our successes, and the list goes on. To find love, we are told to shoot our shots but not to shoot our shots. To position ourselves but not be forceful. To prepare ourselves for love but not come to the table too prepared. We are told that we do too much but not enough. We are criticized for how we wear our hair, how we dress, talk, act... you name it and we've heard it. The marketing aimed at single Black women is geared towards encouraging us to find a problem within ourselves so we can buy a solution; buy into a get-a-man-quick scheme.

While we crawl our way through the marketing pond of scum, we must also navigate the low media representation and portrayal of healthy Black love. This leaves many of us pondering and asking, "What is wrong with me, and will I ever get married?"

For Black Christian women, the landscape is made even more unbearable by the positioning of marriage and singleness in the church.

Singles Christian conferences constantly market the same cookie-cutter messages and unhelpful rhetoric to single women: *"How to Become Better Prepared and Positioned to be Found"* and *"How to be Single and Content in Your Singleness."* Sometimes, I wonder if there is some secret meeting where the agenda is set by Christian conference leaders on which topics to discuss at their annual conferences.

To make the situation even more unnerving, single Christians have a biblical understanding that we are to abstain from sex until marriage. However, the pulpit does not provide any practical ways to implement this truth. Church leaders don't talk about what we should do when we get horny or how to overcome porn addictions. And we rarely hear messages or receive resources aimed at helping Christian singles overcome past sexual trauma. Instead, we are often left to figure out the hard things on our own.

Even when I wasn't attending church services or a singles' conference, I would still see questions such as, "You say you want to be married but are you even ready?" This persistent question of "are you ready" often insinuated there was something more I needed to be doing in order to be found.

It seemed like most people had an obligation to check my motive for marriage. Was it pure? Was it godly? Did my motive center on Christ? Most often than not, I would leave these conversations and conferences confused, discouraged, and feeling hopeless.

Is it wrong to desire marriage? Was I thinking about marriage too much? Was marriage even for me?

Take the sentiments from the secular world on how to be found as a single woman, add the twisting and manipulation of scripture, the one-sided single women's conferences, and God's desire for us to abstain from sex until marriage, then add in the racism, beauty standards, colorism, you name it, and it is no wonder that single Black and single Black Christian women are left pulling out our hair and wondering about the way forward.

Phew! Are you over it yet?

Because I am! I'm sure you feel worn out and confused by the questioning and badgering by family members and strangers about your relationship status. You're tired of having to explain the type of men you've encountered, why the last guy ghosted you, why you didn't choose the last oh-so-eligible man that chose you, and what you plan to do with your eggs if you don't find love in the next 60 days. You desire to be in a healthy, romantic, and loving marriage, and the constant questioning does not make your singleness any easier.

I wrote this book as a safe space to dialogue with you because I was you. Heck, I *am* you.

Like you, I was battling so many questions amid my singleness and abstinence journey. Questions such as, "What do I do when I am horny and need someone to talk me off the ledge?" or "How do I maintain my peace of mind as a single woman while I watch my friends and Instagram cousins get engaged, married, and having children?" "Is marriage even in the books for me?"

The questions were countless, and the answers were few. Unfortunately, I realized that I had no one partnering with me on the journey. And to make matters worse, I saw little to no examples of other people living victoriously while abstaining from sex. Aside from the Black Love docu-series on the OWN Network and a few married friends, I had little to no examples of healthy Black marriages.

I strongly value transparency, but unfortunately, I could not find it in many of the examples I saw. I wanted to know how others were struggling and managing their real-life sex, abstinence, and relationship issues.

I spent much of my earlier Christian days confused. I needed God to give me clarity, and He eventually did. This clarity is what I want to share with you through this book. If I should break this down into three powerful lessons I learned, it would be the following:

- My desire for marriage is perfect in God's eyes.
- If I desire marriage, God will fulfill it.
- If my desire for marriage is not from God, He will remove it.

The title of this book is called "**Ready Set Wait,**" and I wrote it because I want to burst the bubble that says something is wrong with us or that we need to work on ourselves or become better in order to find a spouse. I want to stop the "how are you preparing to be a wife?" rhetoric in its tracks, because I strongly believe that we shouldn't spend our single season solely focused on being a wife or getting ourselves ready or fixed for a man to notice and choose us.

Those are important steps. However, the single's journey has so much more to do with us and our relationship with God and the purpose for which He created us, in and beyond marriage. I reached a point in my single journey where I knew I wanted God to arrange my marriage. I also knew that for that to happen, I'd have to wait on Him. If you are reading this book, I am assuming you have decided that you want to include God in your season of singlehood and are willing to trust God to bring you and your spouse together. If yes, then you are in the right place!

I'll be honest; I don't have all the answers, but I can say that after almost a decade of exploring sex, singleness, and abstinence, I know enough. Plus, whatever I don't cover in the pages of this book, I believe the Holy Spirit will reveal to you. I want this book to be your abstinence accountability partner as you navigate this season. I pray that you will be encouraged to know that you are not alone, you are not crazy, and there is hope for you. Get ready to heal from past trauma, receive God's love, get answers to the questions you have, and whatever else God wants to get to you through the pages of this book.

This book did not land in your hands by happenstance, this was divinely given to you. Whether you stumbled on it at a bookstore, a friend gifted it to you, or you were motivated to purchase it for yourself; this book and the message in it are for you.

1

God, Why Am I Still Single?

It was the first week at my new job. I was working on a PowerPoint presentation when my thoughts were interrupted by loud, excited screams.

"You have to tell our Senior Vice President the great news," I overheard the vice president saying, "you know she loves this stuff."

"Let me guess, someone just got engaged," I thought.

Just then, my newly engaged co-worker run over to my cubicle, beaming with excitement. "I just got engaged," she said.

"Congratulations," I replied, managing to smile. "I...didn't know you were dating." What I was really thinking was, *I don't even know you and I don't care. This can't be what my life has come to.*

Oh, but this was my life!

Everyone around me was getting engaged and married. It didn't help that I was spending endless hours scrolling through Instagram and living vicariously through those who were living picture-perfect, married lives. It felt like peeling a scab off an open wound and then picking at it. It grieved my spirit every time another engagement popped up on my screen.

To ease the pain, I took weeks off from social media because I was overwhelmed by all the images of marriages, bridal showers, baby showers, gender reveals, and proposals. I was tired of being reminded that I was single.

Heck, I was tired of being single.

I was tired of being asked, "Why are you still single?"

I was tired of having to explain why I was still single.

I was tired of doing single people things.

I was tired of having single friends.

I was tired of seeing single memes.

I was tired of singles' conferences.

I was simply tired of being tired of being single!

I have reached this point multiple times in my period of singleness, and I often ask God, "God, why am I still single?"

How many times have you asked this same question of God?

There were times when I thought something was wrong with me. Times when I thought I needed to work on myself so I could find a spouse. Times when I settled rather than waited. When I settled, I wasn't even looking for someone to complete me. I had thrown away the concept of "better half," and was just ready for love. I was lonely, and I craved companionship.

I wanted to start my own family. One of the hardest parts about journeying through singleness is feeling alone. Not just feeling physically alone but also feeling alone in our situation. We think, "No one feels the way I feel," or "No one else is going through this." We often wonder why this is happening to us. These are common conversations I've had with other single women. Living in this digital age only makes loneliness feel worse. These feelings can be further exacerbated by counsel that sometimes makes us feel like we are doing it all wrong.

People kept saying, "He comes when you stop looking," but that didn't help, because I have had seasons where I didn't look and still nothing happened. Still, the worst advice I've heard on why I am still single is any advice given on why I am still single. The only one who holds the answer to this question is God

I believe that God can lead us individually to the truth of why we're still single; there is no one answer for everyone. There may be reasons why God has not yet opened the door of marriage for us, and I do have insights into two reasons why. Neither one of those reasons says it's because there's something wrong with you.

I. You are in the wrong relationship.

I was in a relationship for seven years. For six out of those seven years, I didn't know who I was. My ex-boyfriend and I started dating when I was 19 years old, so I grew into a woman in my relationship with him. So much of what I enjoyed in life was with and through him. Although I had friends, most of my time was spent with him. This meant that all of the places I enjoyed going to, I enjoyed going to with him. Most of the hobbies I developed, I developed with him. My favorite foods, restaurants, and places to visit were all connected to my relationship with him.

Simply put, he was a huge part of my life, and my expectation without question was that we'd get married. But we didn't get married. Actually, we fell apart.

The truth is, I never put my relationship in God's hands. I never once said: "God, if he's the one, tell me or show me!" Instead, I was planning a marriage in my head based on my own will. It was a relationship I put together and had to keep working to put together while God was allowing it to fall apart. It was not a relationship ordained by God. How did I know? The relationship didn't lead me any closer to Him. Any relationship where God has become less of a priority is not of God, rather it is an idol.

Oftentimes we idolize relationships because we cannot picture ourselves alone even when the relationship is toxic. I often felt unloved in my relationships, but the thought of someone else loving me and loving me well was far from my mind. I thought the love I was receiving, or lack thereof, from my ex-boyfriend was all I was worth. I didn't know there was something better than what I was accepting until I was no longer accepting it.

Thankfully, amid my long-term relationship, God saved me. I found Christ and was baptized. I discovered more about myself and God. I began to uncover my purpose and who God created me to be. I could only discover this by developing a relationship with my creator. It was clear that God didn't want me and my ex to get married, although the world around us minimized it to him having commitment issues.

I have had walking visions of what my life would have looked like if I had married my ex. Visions of a dying purpose the minute I said, "I do." I am glad that God saved me. Of course, there were huge red flags in that relationship, but, because I wanted to be married so badly, I did not see them.

Once I was free from the constraints of that relationship, I grew an intimate relationship with God and was able to uncover the parts of me that had been hidden while I was distracted by my relationship. I was also able to heal from the trauma of that relationship. The work of healing hurt, but I am grateful that God is gentle with us.

> He tends his flock like a shepherd: He gathers the lambs in his arms and carries them close to his heart; he gently leads those that have young. (Isaiah 40:11 NIV)

The scripture above describes how gentle our Father is with us, His children. Even when He is preventing us from getting married, it is an act of gentle love; God wants us. He is the shepherd, and we are his flock, his sheep.

The image of God carrying us in His bosom defines the closeness that is possible between humans and God. It is God's desire for us to be near Him; it is intimacy.

After the relationship with my ex ended, I entered many situationships with men whom I prayed would be "the one." The reality was that I didn't understand what marriage meant to God. I didn't know how much He values it, or the role marriage plays in God's kingdom.

I thought marriage was simply a devotion of love to be shared with my spouse for the rest of my life. I had to change my perspective if I expected God to bring me a spouse. Through this journey, God has made it clear to me that it's in my best interest to 1) pray for my spouse, and 2) allow God to prepare me for him as opposed to me trying to fix myself to be worthy of marriage.

The experience with my ex, and the many others after it, also taught me to stop forcing myself on people and to stop sitting at tables where I wasn't welcome. Beyond romantic relationships, I stopped trying to befriend people simply because I felt the need to have a more successful circle of friends to get ahead. I stopped trying to force things that weren't meant for me.

I want to encourage you! If you find yourself in a relationship where you have to lie, hide, minimize yourself, or escape your purpose to keep the relationship, then you should ask God if this is who He wants you to marry. You may not have gotten to a place where you can clearly hear God's voice, and that's okay. I still encourage you to ask God to give you a sign. God speaks in a still small voice, but He also speaks through people – He can speak through anyone and anything. Pray and ask God to show you a clear sign that the person you are with is who He has ordained for you to marry.

Many of you reading this book already know the answer, but sometimes our desires can blind us, leaving us to believe that the wrong one is the right one.

II. God is preparing you to experience His best

My family and close friends know that I prefer a home-cooked meal over a microwaved meal any day. When you are hungry and need to whip together something on the go, a box of Velveeta macaroni and cheese is quite delectable. But nothing beats a homemade macaroni and cheese carefully crafted with love. A meal made with the right ingredients and baked to perfection always hits differently!

The same principle can be true for you in your quest for marriage. You don't want a marriage that is mere 'Instagram goals,' one that is "hot" on the outside and "cold" on the inside. What you want is a marriage prepared and specially crafted by God, with love. When you let God prepare you on his terms, in his timing, you will be better prepared to step into marriage at His right time for you, and on the right foundation.

This is not a clarion call for you to fix yourself so you can be approved for marriage, rather it is a charge to let God continue his work in you in this season until he is ready to reveal you to your significant other. A building's foundation is what makes it stand, and the same goes for a marriage. The foundation of a marriage is God and two individuals with characteristics that align with Him.

Waiting for God's best may lead to years of being hidden by God. Just like a seed is planted, hidden, and watered, God may be doing the same for you. He is hidden you from situationships that will damage you or worst, draw you away from God. If you are being hidden by God, count that as an honor.

It took me a while to learn this truth. For so many years, I thought the reason I wasn't attracting men was that I wasn't attractive when in actuality, it was because God had me hidden in plain sight. Several times, I tried to come out of hiding, only to fall flat on my face with disappointment to then go back into hiding. God adores you so much that He doesn't want the wrong man to see and ruin you.

Sis, you are beautiful. You are a gem. You're precious in God's sight. There's absolutely nothing wrong with you. You're not being overlooked, you're planted. Anything that is planted cannot be seen until it has been watered. Let God continue to water you. Let Him nurture you.

When the time is right, you will sprout from the ground with strong roots. The man God has for you will pick you. You won't have to chase after him and lose yourself to get or keep Him. God is not done with you yet. Trust Him to do a complete work in you. Wait on His time. You may not be married yet and that is okay; when the time comes you and bae will be happy you waited.

REFLECTION

If you are single and desiring marriage, know that the journey is not always easy. You may find yourself wondering if love will ever find you. While these thoughts run rampant through your mind, there will be people willing and ready to antagonize you about your relationship status. I'm in the same boat as you, so I understand.

My goal is not to make you feel any worse about your situation but rather to encourage you to reflect on a few things. Are you single because you are in the wrong relationship, or are you single because God has you hidden?

It may be for some other reasons that only God can reveal to you if he so chooses. But whatever the reason may be, know that there is no question that God cannot answer and no clarity He cannot give. Remember this!

LET'S PRAY

Heavenly Father, we come before you to give you the thanks and praise you deserve. We thank you for being both our Lord and our God. You are a father to those who are fatherless and a friend to those who are friendless. We can search the world and we will not find anyone that compares to you. You are the alpha and the omega, and you know and care about everything that happens in our midst. You will not leave us alone or without, and this includes ensuring we are not ignorant of your plans.

Your word says that your Holy Spirit leads us into all truths. Where you are, darkness cannot exist. We thank you for being the light in our lives and illuminating the paths we are to walk. We thank you for directing and ordering our footsteps so that we don't head in the wrong direction. Thank you for not holding anything against us when we have strayed from your plans and gone the wrong way.

You died that we may have access to unlimited unforgiveness. We ask for it now and we repent from our wrongdoings. Thank you for forgiving us and giving us chance after chance after chance. We petition you to help us make good decisions in our relationships. We ask that you send us down the right path, Lord. If we are in any relationship that is not of you, we give you permission to step in and give us a sign.

If our relationships are not ordained, please help us to leave. You say in your word that you do not tempt us beyond that which we can handle and for every temptation, you give us a way out. Thank you, Lord, for a clear escape route. Thank you for not leaving us alone in this. If we have to leave, give us the strength to do so.

We thank you for being our rearguard to go behind us and protect us. We desire to do your will with confidence knowing you have our best interest at heart. We thank you for perfecting your will in us and manifesting the desires of our hearts in Jesus' name. Amen.

2.

Am I *Even* Worthy to Be Loved?

"Sade, what does love mean to you?"

"Huh?" Here goes God again asking questions.

"What does love mean to you?" He repeated.

When God asked the question, I was almost afraid to respond because I wasn't sure I knew the answer. Yes, I want to be married. Yes, I desire a husband. But shockingly, I had not considered what *love* would look like in a marriage. It made me wonder how I received love and expected to be loved.

I reflected on my past relationships and situationships, and I realized that I dated based on my warped definition of my own worthiness. When I look back at the men I let into the intimate parts of me, I recognized that I dated based on what I thought I deserved. I accepted scraps because I thought I was worth scraps.

I was willing to accept the breadcrumbs I was handed because anything was better than nothing. I spent time with men who wasted my time even when I knew they were not willing to commit. Men who came around during my most vulnerable times and who often distracted me and made matters worse. I spent hours talking to many who didn't offer up plans for a date. Men who told me they weren't interested in talking to me because I was abstaining. Even married men have tried to cheat on their wives with me, leaving me feeling like all I was worth was someone else's scraps.

Sis, I've dealt with my share of disappointing situations, and I am sure you have too.

Often, I would look in the mirror and ask God if something was wrong with me. I questioned whether I was attractive because men wouldn't look at me. I considered getting body adjustments so I could look more appealing. I hid my personality with the hopes that becoming more timid, quieter, and less ambitious would attract men. But nothing I considered doing or did, changed the circumstances. So I learned to endure being single and all the emotions that came with it.

It's hard to wait on the one when it seems like there is no "one" available. As a Black woman, I've heard all the dreary statistics. One in three black men are imprisoned, over 50% are gay, another percentage are married, and the rest are not ready to commit, or something of that nature. If you're a Black woman, I am sure you have heard the numbers too, and it has probably left you wondering if there is anyone out there for you. Knowing I only need one husband brings some assurance and relief. Though the petty parts of me believe we've all waited long enough to be blessed with two. Don't you think?

Anyway, as I wrestled with my dissatisfaction with my physical body, my feelings of being overlooked, and the emotions around being single, there was a much bigger war simmering beneath. This war was happening on the battlefield of my mind, it was the inner dialogue I was having with myself about my worth and whether I deserved love.

The adversary (Satan) took that doubt and played me with it. I am sure many of you have been here, and you may still be wrestling with phrases like: "I am not worth it," "No one loves me," and "I will never find love."

Sis, I am here to tell you that these are all lies from Satan, and we must start, and continue, to counter the enemy's lies with the truth.

So what is the truth? The truth is in the word of God. We all have our own false definitions of what love means, but regardless of how we feel about love and how we have been loved in our past relationships, the real and truest definition of love is found in God's word.

So, to answer the question God asked me, "What does love mean to me?"

Love is unconditional.

When I think about the most outward act of love, I think about Jesus' death.

God loved us so much that He gave, He sacrificed.

Love is willing to make sacrifices, for the better good; even when it hurts.

Love doesn't seek to please itself; it is not self-serving...

As I wrote down what love meant to me, I noticed that the words that first flowed from my heart were God's definition of love in 1 Corinthians 13, and he began to encourage me with the truth of the scripture. When I was writing, I felt a deep connection with the truth as the Holy Spirit began to minister to me. I understood the sacrifice Jesus made on my behalf, and on yours, and I perceived the parallels in marriage. The hard truths of God's love displayed in sacrifice were spoken softly to me as I continued to write:

Love is a choice. An outward act, not an inward tingling feeling.

Love looks to the future benefit, it hopes.

Love is eternal and everlasting (the love of God).

Love does not abandon when someone does wrong...

"*Love does not abandon when someone does wrong*" hit home for me because as you journey with me through this book, you will learn that abandonment and rejection were some of the issues I had to overcome. In the past, when I felt the sting of rejection and abandonment, or disloyalty coming, I would run. Running was my escape, my way of protecting myself. The moment those words, "Love does not abandon when someone does wrong" left my fingertips, I instinctively knew the root.

As simple as it may sound to some, I realized that those who left and abandoned me did not do so because I was unlovable. Their actions had less to do with me and more to do with their character. I wasn't unlovable. I wasn't unworthy. These were the words that I had to constantly affirm myself with. Not because they were the truth based on my own intellect but because these were the truths God believed about me.

Love survives trials and tribulations.

Love does not cease at someone's faults, it actually loves them through it, past it, and over it.

Love isn't jealous or envious.

Love is redeeming.

Love covers all wrongs.

It doesn't mask wrongs; it drives out wrongs.

Love drives out evil.

Love compromises.

Love bends, it is flexible.

Love doesn't crack.

Love lasts even when problems arise.

Love is not based on the existence of perfect conditions. Love is unconditional.

Love survives time.

Love is warm, a safe haven, it's enveloping and secure.

Love is safe.

Love doesn't have to prove itself.

Love isn't prideful or egotistical.

Love is."

As you read these words, you may picture the love of a spouse or a significant other. While a lot of this can be experienced in a romantic relationship, this is the picture of God's love for you. The truth is that you are loved and valued. You are worth it. You are deserving. You are enough. You are that chick, not because of you or anything you have done or are doing or will do.

You are deserving and worthy simply because God says so. The truth is that even though we don't deserve anything from God, He still chose us and proclaims that we are his prized jewels. He highlighted that love and truth by paying an ultimate price; He gave up his life so that we can have life. That is the love you deserve and have.

> Greater love has no one than this: to lay down one's life for one's friends. (John 15:13)

But he didn't stop at laying down His life, He also chose to reside within us. As such, we are his temple; He chose us. We are seen, the almighty God never overlooks us. Whenever you feel invisible, you can declare it is a lie. God sees us and chooses us.

Sis, do you not know that *you are fearfully and wonderfully made in God's image* (Psalm 139:4)?

My journey to finding the true meaning of love led me to discover that I sought validation from men rather than from God. The reason why I found myself in so many unfavorable situationships was that I didn't know how much God loved me. I didn't understand what God's love looked like although I'd read and heard about it through others. Not understanding God's love was a foundational pillar in how I knew to receive love.

Anchoring in the truth of God's love enables us to yearn for so much more in the relationships we choose. If we continue to base our worth on what people say about us or how they treat us or even how we allow them to treat us, we will stay in a position of hopelessness. When we jump into relationships because we are overwhelmed by our fear of being alone, we will continue to attach our purpose, happiness, and peace to another individual.

Let me share another truth with you. Your purpose is already in you and your joy is in God and God alone. A relationship cannot mend the broken pieces in your life, and it cannot heal you, make you happy, or make you whole. Only God can do that.

Your worth is not based on someone's inability to see it; your worth is in Christ and what he says about you. After God created the earth, He looked out and said that everything was good. That includes you! The hairs on your head are numbered, God was concerned about the details when He created you. This is the work that God wants to do in us, and I believe this is more important than anything that will transpire in a marriage.

We are all deserving of a love that curls our toes and steadies our hearts. A love that is dependable and warm. A love that sacrifices and romances. Recognizing that the love of Christ does all this and more is the difference between hearing about God's love versus experiencing it.

I would like to challenge you to sit in scripture and imagine all of the love God shared, as he wildly pursues after the heart of humankind. It is the very same love you are receiving from your Heavenly Father today.

REFLECTION

When God first asked me what love was, I was taken aback. Since then, I have learned to truly understand what 1 Corinthians 13 means.

To understand love, we must know how God defines it. 1 Corinthians 13 will always be the hallmark for the definition of love for me, as it should be for all believers. It is a place of reference for us.

So just as the Father asked me what love meant to me, I am challenging you to answer this too. When you think about love, what first comes to your mind? If your thoughts of love do not line up with God's definition of it, perhaps this calls for a deeper level of exploring with God.

LET'S PRAY

Father God, we come before you today because we need you! We need your love to illuminate the lies we've believed about love and our worth. We recognize that you are the power greater than us, and we thank you for your strength.

We thank you because when we are at our weakest or lowest points, we can count on you. We thank you because you promise to never put us through anything that won't work out for our good. Although we may have been rejected, pushed to the side; overlooked; devalued; and abandoned, we can seek and find healing in You! There is no issue we face that is too hard for you to handle.

We give every issue to you today. Heal our broken hearts. Your word says that a broken spirit and a contrite heart you will never despise. Thank you, Lord, for never turning your back on us. Heal us, Lord. Seek the deepest wounds of our hearts and begin the healing process so that we can be whole.

From this day forward, we will walk in the beauty and confidence that you see when you see us. Thank you for this opportunity to shine the light on the dark areas of our life and thank you for your healing power and your love.

In Jesus' name. Amen.

3.

God, You Abandoned Me

When I was four, my mother abandoned me and my father. My father had cirrhosis of the liver and diabetes and still managed to raise me alone, until his health began to decline three years into our journey as a family of two. I avoided the foster care system narrowly when my paternal aunt stepped up and took me in. While my mom and I have since developed an amazing relationship, being abandoned by a parent comes with its share of trauma. I repressed most of it over the years, and when it rose to the surface years later, I was shocked.

The first time it resurfaced, I was sitting with my cousin at the end of a Mother's Day church service when an overwhelming feeling of sadness came over me. All around me, I watched the faces of the mothers light up as their daughters and sons presented them with hugs and flowers. Tears began to run down my eyes and quickly turned uncontrollable. My younger cousin tried to console me, but I couldn't articulate how I was feeling. What was it that triggered me? My mother and I had an amazing relationship at that point, so I didn't understand why I was feeling sad on Mother's Day.

It wasn't until I arrived home that The Holy Spirit revealed what had happened to me. I'd never forgiven my mother for abandoning me. It didn't make sense, so I began to question God.

"How is this possible?" I asked.

"I'm healed from what my mother did," I thought.

"We have a great relationship," I said.

It was then that I realized that although the relationship had been re-established, I had never taken the time to process how her actions affected me. I had never verbalized or processed the fact that I never allowed myself to forgive her for what she'd done.

I speak to a lot of women who struggle with bitterness, resentment, and unforgiveness. Maybe you too have been hurt, abandoned, or rejected by someone. I want you to take a moment to reflect on whether or not you've allowed yourself the time to address how that affected you. Have you identified exactly what happened to you and how it has made you feel? Do you feel free?

In my case, rejection and abandonment had cast themselves as shadows over my life. They were the driving forces behind a lot of the destructive decisions I made in relationships and friendships. I found myself in cycles of falling deeply in lust with men I had no synergy or compatibility with.

I can recall many times when I sought validation from men. I desired for a man to see me the way I couldn't see myself. I was desperate for love and chose to couple up with men I was not equally yoked with, men who were unsaved and who were unwilling to commit. I wanted to feel wanted, needed and valued. Then right before I could get hurt, I'd force myself to emotionally detach. I pulled the victim card often to justify my behavior. This pattern in relationships was synonymous with patterns in my friendships as well.

However painful the waiting season and the revelations in this season have been, I am grateful that God allowed me to experience them. I am even more grateful that he transformed my mind into believing and knowing that I don't need a man or a relationship to validate me. I don't recall when the lightbulb came on, but once I saw myself the way that God sees me, I began to value myself and my actions started to align with those values. I am no longer the 4-year-old girl who was abandoned and felt rejected. I deserved to be loved, and that love started with God and me and even that wasn't an easy journey.

When we speak about abandonment and rejection issues, it's usually in our relationship with other individuals, but what about when we feel rejected and abandoned by God? It is one thing to recognize that I felt abandoned and rejected by my parents, and to understand how that played out in my life, especially in relationships and friendships. It was definitely another thing to recognize and verbalize that I felt rejected and abandoned by God. That I felt God brought me to wars and abandoned me right in the middle of them. When I looked at how others were progressing and obtaining the desires of my heart, it made me feel forgotten by God. I often asked, "God, do you even see me?" "Do my tears mean nothing to you?" "Am I praying amiss?"

Whenever I shared this with others, I was met with surprise and pushback. "God can never abandon you," people were quick to say, but sometimes it sure can feel like He has, that He did abandon me. I felt this way because even though there are multiple verses in scripture where God assures us that He will never leave us nor forsake us, the trajectory of my life didn't feel like these scripture verses. Many would say I needed a mental reset, and I did. But what I also needed to do was to go before God, just as I am, and lay my feelings before Him, whether those feelings were valid or not, true or not.

Unfortunately, in many Christian communities, there are directives on how to talk to God and some can lean into stiff and disingenuous. We often find it easier to address how others have made us feel, but we hold back from "keeping it real" with God about how He makes or made us feel. I believe God wants us to be transparent, open, and honest with Him.

Many don't know they can come to God with their transparent, open, and honest feelings and points of view, and several factors contribute to how we exist in a relationship with God. We may have been taught to wear masks dressed up as reverence before God. We are afraid God will strike us if we tell Him we feel let down by Him.

We believe revering God is more important than being honest about our feelings before Him.

When I read Hebrews 4:16 *"Let us, therefore, come boldly to the throne of grace, that we may obtain mercy and find grace to help in time of need,"* I often wonder what a bold stance would look like. Can we come to God boldly if we leave our feelings hidden from Him? Don't you know that God knows what you want and need before your mind can fathom it? Do you not know that everything you feel He also feels? Do you not understand that there is nothing that you can hide from Him? So why aren't we honest about how we feel towards Him?

How we show up in our communication with God can be the difference between religion and relationship. As you journey on your walk of faith, you will realize the importance of being in direct and honest communication with God. Churchianity, better known as legalism (religiosity) will make you feel that each time you speak to God you need to hide your disappointment or frustration from Him. It will make you feel as if you can't be completely raw with God about how you feel. All of which is untrue.

God knows your thoughts. He knows how you will respond to situations. He knows how you feel about what has transpired in your life. He understands your frustrations even when you can't articulate them in words. Don't let religiosity keep you from building a true relationship with your Heavenly Father. If you need to scream or yell to get out your raw and honest feelings with God, then do that. Remove the mask, Sis, and let God get to the heart of the issue with you.

It is often said that relationships are strengthened in times of adversity, and I found this to be true. Faith that is not tested is not faith they say, I also find this to be true. What do we do when we feel like God has overlooked our request for love? What do we do when we feel like we are praying for God to bring us a spouse and yet, it is year five and we are still single? What do we do? At the least, bring your grievances to God. We can pretend with the world, but we cannot and should not hide our faces from an omniscient and omnipresent God.

So, in the moments of my greatest trials, I learned to be honest about how I felt. I often was left with no choice, but to tell God exactly how I was feeling:

God, I feel like you've rejected me.

I feel like you have left me alone in this.

I feel like you have closed your ears to my prayers.

I feel alone.

I feel left out of your plans.

I feel illegitimate.

These are all real feelings, and it is important to tap into how you feel and express them. For the longest time, the primary descriptor I had for my feelings was, "I am angry." I have learned that I have not been just angry, but I have also felt let down, I have felt rejected, I have felt overlooked, I have felt like I've been given the short end of the stick, and I have felt unloved and undervalued by God.

REFLECTION

Disappointment, rejection, and abandonment have been commonplace for me, have they for you? Can you too identify with the experiences of being left, rejected, and let down? I'm sure many of you reading this can.

Sis, you are not alone. I truly want to encourage you to find rest in being honest with God about how you feel. There is so much freedom in removing the mask of religiosity and getting real with God. When you "get real" with God, you permit Him to step into those parts of your life you've tried to hide. This is where your relationship with Him deepens. Can I pray for you?

LET'S PRAY

Blessed Father, you love us so much that you invite us into fellowship with you. My sister, reading this, needs to know that it's okay to be naked before you Lord. Help her to be free from the shame that has kept her from being honest with you.

I pray that she will see and experience the true love of you Father. May she know that this love comes with acceptance and not condemnation. You see her. Help her to truly understand this. You desire her unadulterated feelings, help her to believe this. I pray that the love of God will completely overtake her at this moment.

May she surrender every thought that exalts itself over the knowledge of who you are and find rest.

4.

Dealing with Disappointment

Disappointment has been a common thread in my journey through singleness. Although, it wasn't easily identifiable at the onset. Proverbs 13:12a says *Hope deferred makes the heart sick...* This is exactly what disappointment felt like to me. The definition of disappointment is feeling sad, unhappy, or displeased because something was not as good as expected or because something you hoped for or expected did not happen. It was easier to acknowledge anger than disappointment!

If I could maintain my pride, I wouldn't have to admit that I felt hurt by what another person had done to me. I wanted to maintain my tough girl persona; I didn't want to wear my heart on my sleeve.

But what causes us to hide behind these tough girls and #unbothered personas? Mine started as a little girl. Growing up in my home, the rules were the rules. We couldn't disagree with the rules, have a question about it, or let alone express an opinion! Am I alone in this? We did what we were told and that was that. When it came to my feelings, what were those? I wasn't allowed to have feelings. Not that it makes it right, but my parents did the best they could and now I have to unlearn a lot of it.

There was this one incident where I came home from school in anger. I burst through the front door and headed straight to a bookcase on which sat a bundle of pencils. I took the pencils off the bookcase and broke them in half, all 50 something of them. I was hurting and crying out for attention and help. Instead of consoling me and inquiring why I was acting out, I was met with discipline.

This was a constant pattern in my home. As an adult, I had a hard time identifying my disappointment. I'd repressed feelings for so long that I couldn't identify how I felt. My dad would constantly tell me to "be strong" whenever he saw me crying. I learned that strength was in my ability to hold in how I felt, this was being strong but "I was strong and wrong."

It becomes second nature for us to carry these learnings into adult friendships and relationships. We find ourselves being proud for not feeling. We pride ourselves on not feeling any emotion after a breakup when, in actuality, we were disappointed. Instead of acknowledging that we feel let down, we hide behind anger. Anger is such a prideful emotion because it makes us feel powerful, and it makes us feel strong. We say things like: "I'm okay," "I'm not bothered," "I don't care," or "It is what it is." We live in a *ghosting* culture, so closure isn't always accessible. We often feel as though we have to find closure on our own because expecting the other individual to understand and acknowledge how they made us feel may be unrealistic.

In order for me to overcome disappointment, I had to consciously pinpoint how people made me feel. A good friend encouraged me to slowly start to discern my emotions and outwardly express them with words. Thank you, Destiny. Being in a state of constantly repressing my feelings made it hard for me to identify how I felt. I had to learn to put language to my anger. I was no longer allowed to say: I am angry but rather – "I feel let down and disappointed."

When I started online dating, I was met with countless disappointments. Not only did the disappointment come from unmet expectations in my relationships and "situationships," but I also became disappointed in God. Feeling disappointed with God felt just like feeling abandoned by God; it is a real feeling. What I love about God is that, again, He understands our feelings and He desires that we bring these feelings to Him.

How many times have you been there in your singleness? How many times have you wondered why God decided to bless everyone with marriage, but you? How often have you wondered if God has forgotten you? Disappointment is a real feeling and God understands it.

I realized that I was disappointed and that no matter how much I prayed, lived for God, fasted, and obeyed him, I had not got what I desired – a marriage. Of course, I knew obedience did not necessarily lead to marriage nor does not being married mean that God loved me less. Many of us hide behind masks of "I'm blessed and highly favored" while feeling disappointed.

No matter how blessed we are and how faithful we may be, disappointment is a real emotion, and we can learn a healthy way to deal with it. The first step is to identify and acknowledge it and the second is to allow God to walk through it with you. God can heal your heart from disappointment, but first, you need to answer this question: why are you disappointed and who disappointed you? When disappointment rises to the surface, I know I can have an open and honest conversation with God about how I feel, or simply cry until I feel better.

In your season of waiting, I hope that you have an opportunity to work through these repressed events. You do not have to do it alone. Let God purge you; take out the mess, the hurt, the pain, the disappointments, the regrets, the resentments. Let Him take everything that is needed to be removed out of you so that the foundation on which you build your future marriage can be strong.

We carry around so much baggage from our past. For me, it was loads of disappointment, abandonment, and rejection. I carried this until God stepped in. You can let him step in too. As you journey through your singleness, you will discover some things about yourself that will blow your mind, and everything isn't pretty. The goal is to let God uncover the mess, heal the pain, and deliver you from the shame. Healing from disappointment does not happen overnight but you have to start somewhere. What's the best way to start? Invite God into these areas of your life.

REFLECTION

You may be carrying around the weight of trauma. Maybe rejection, abandonment, and disappointment are not the issues that torment you, but I encourage you to lean into the issues and blocks you have.

How do you feel about being single? What *really* bothers you about your current circumstance?

Are you ready to acknowledge it? Are you ready to get to the core of how you feel? You don't just feel lonely, you may feel unworthy to be loved. You may feel undervalued. You may feel unlovable.

Whatever you feel, talk about it; release it. Therefore, go boldly to the throne of grace, that YOU may obtain mercy and find grace to help YOU in your time of need.

LET'S PRAY

God, my life has been plagued by disappointments too many to be numbered. I have felt the sting of being let down over and over. There are times that I've hidden my true emotions from you out of fear of judgment or your wrath, but not today. God, I lay the weight of disappointment at your feet.

You instruct us in Your Word to come boldly to the throne of grace that we may obtain the mercy to help us in our time of need. Right now is my time of need and I am coming to you with bold confidence.

Thank you, Lord, for replacing my dismay with joy. Thank you for restoring my faith in your love for me. Thank you for allowing me to let go of the weight that I've been carrying.

I pray that I will not leave this moment without receiving your comfort, grace, strength, and endurance to wait on you.

In Jesus' name. Amen.

5.

Letting Go of the Hurt

My father was the first person I told after I was molested. The details of the molestation are vague, but my earliest memories are of being violated. My sexual desires were heightened as a result. I was tormented by constant sexual thoughts, thoughts an undeveloped youth shouldn't be forced to live with.

This opened the door to sexual perversion and pornography addiction. My addiction to pornography led to pre-marital sex, anger, unforgiveness, and shame. At the onset, pornography seemed like an escape for me, but it quickly brought on the weight of shame and oppression. I never felt good after each act, and I carried the sting of the shame around with me for years. I didn't think I could break free from it.

But God, by His grace, delivered me. He gave me grace in my single season to process and heal. Two significant events happened that paved the way for healing from much of the baggage I was carrying.

Forgiveness - If "unforgiveness only hurts you," were a person, then I am that person. I'm a real-life testament to the truth that not forgiving the people who hurt you will hold you captive, not them. Unforgiveness was the one thing I had to hold on to; it was the power I could wield, but it became a prison. The more I held onto "who did what to me," the more the prison walls closed in. Unforgiveness holds another captive in your mind and heart, it keeps you in a cell. I closed myself off to people, love, and God. My pride and resentment was a sting that only I felt, but it had also become my only defense.

I played victim because of my abandonment and rejection issues and the trauma from molestation. In addition, I'd allowed bitterness to seep into my heart, and it built an added layer of fortified walls around the prison I was already in, and it kept at bay those I feared would disappoint me. My pride often said, "I don't wanna get played" so I learned to cut "you" off before you hurt me. I felt like disappointment was all I knew until God began chipping away at the walls.

I didn't know how to forgive, but I soon learned that forgiveness was a choice. We cannot change what we've experienced but, through the power of God, we can work through it. The truth was, I wanted friendship and love, but all my issues stood in the way. I knew I could either stay bitter or get better. I chose to get better and decided to forgive the people who had hurt me starting with my ex.

For years after our breakup, I was plagued with demonic and dark dreams about our relationship. I would have sexual dreams about my ex-boyfriend which made me constantly relive our relationship. I would wake up and pray that God would take the dreams away. After several years of having these dreams, I realized that I couldn't pray them away. I asked God to show me what I needed to do, and He simply said "forgive."

What seemed like an easy concept turned out to be more difficult than I thought. I realized that I didn't know how to forgive. You see, I held myself back for years because my ex-boyfriend left me to date a mutual friend of ours. At first, I thought I didn't care, but in reality, my pride didn't want to feel the hurt. I didn't want to acknowledge that I felt yet again rejected and abandoned. How could I maintain my "image" and be disappointed at the same time? I refused to.

With the help of a friend, I realized that in order to forgive, I needed to choose to pray for him. So one day, I stood in my shower as the tears ran down my face and I choked over the words: "I forgive him, I forgive her." I went on to bless their union. I prayed for their hearts and asked that God would give them the love they desired. The dreams ceased.

Forgiveness is a choice, and I was the only person being hurt by choosing unforgiveness. In the process of forgiving them, I realized three things:

1. Anger was an easier emotion because I could maintain the "power."

2. Anger was my way of controlling my feelings.

3. Accepting the disappointment and hurt of rejection felt like losing control.

Forgiveness is not dependent on an apology from the offender. You don't have to wait to hear the words "sorry," before you forgive. You can still have peace and closure by choosing to forgive. Are you ready to forgive and let go?

Letting Go! - The second significant event that paved the way for my healing journey was letting go of my past. From a societal perspective, there is often a negative connotation surrounding death. The death of a loved one is a physical separation between us and them, but for believers, death brings **us closer to oneness and true wholeness with Christ**.

God's word says that we are simply sojourning through this life; the complex aspect of sojourning are the things we face and experience.

"For we are strangers before you and sojourners, as all our fathers were. Our days on the earth are like a shadow, and there is no abiding," (1 Chronicles 29:15 ESV).

The woman I was back then was very different from the woman I am today. And although I don't regret anything that I did back then, I am grateful that I no longer live my life recklessly.

I not only attended college (State College) in Pennsylvania, but I also met my ex-boyfriend there. After we left State College, my friends often went back to visit, but I always stayed back because there was nothing there for me. Every path I thought my life would take when I was in college, didn't happen. The relationship that I believed would lead to marriage, didn't. The friendships I had built, and thought would last forever, ended. The career path I chose and invested thousands of dollars into, crumbled before my eyes.

Then, about ten years or so after I graduated, I connected with a group of older and wise women who resided at State College. My connection with them was far different from my past connections with the school. Subsequently, I received another invitation to visit

State College, and, this time, I had to look deep within myself to analyze my initial hesitation. What was it that was keeping me from visiting this place? That's when it hit me; it was disappointment.

I had to come face-to-face with that disappointment. The disappointment that my life had turned out differently from what it once was. I battled with whether or not God wanted me to take this trip. Was there something I needed to face head-on at State College? Was there something there that I needed to conquer or overcome? Why now, after 10 years do I have another invitation to visit a place I had been resisting for years? I stepped out on faith, booked a ticket, and headed to State College PA. Before I left, I had a conversation with God in which He assured me that my trip would be more than I expected but exactly what I needed.

On the first day of my arrival at my alma mater, a butterfly landed on our car. At that moment, I knew that God was speaking to me, even if I wasn't quite sure exactly what He was saying. Not only did the butterfly land on the car, but it also stayed on the windshield and refused to leave.

As we started to drive off, 10-15-20 mph the butterfly braced itself against the wind and held on tight. I hit the windshield hoping it would let go and fly off because I didn't want to see its demise, but the faster we drove, and the harder I hit, the firmer it stayed planted.

So later that night, I prayed, took out my journal, and asked God, "God, what is it that you wanted to teach me through this butterfly." And God spoke, "A butterfly indicates change – complex and unique. No two butterflies are identical. What am I doing in you is a new thing, something that hasn't been done before?"

"God, why did the butterfly hold on to the windshield for so long?"

"Embrace change. Trust me in this. Sometimes, you may need a little push, but you will soar just like that butterfly. I sent it as a sign to indicate transformation. This is what this trip was for you. I wanted to show you how much you've changed; it was no coincidence that you saw the butterfly on your first day. I speak through everything. Look for the signs. Hold tight to the newly transformed you. There is nothing to fear. This place is significant for you; this is where the old things died for you. This is why you had to come back, especially now. Think about Lazarus and his grave clothes. He came up out of them, just like you."

State College was the place where the old me died.

After that encounter with God, the story of Lazarus became very significant for me.

In the book of John, Jesus called out to Lazarus in a loud voice, "Lazarus, come out!" The dead man came out, his hands and feet wrapped with strips of linen, and a cloth around his face. Jesus said to them, "Take off the grave clothes and let him go." (John 11:43-44)

What is the significance of the removal of grave clothing? I would like to assume that grave clothing symbolizes where he came from, but God wanted the world to know that he had been given new life. Grave clothes can be symbolic of baggage.

What are the things and people that you are willing to leave in the grave where they belong? Can I encourage you to leave all the dead things behind? Let God do the transformation in you. Let Him raise you from the dead and present you to the world as a new creature. If you love God, you can trust that He has great things in store for you. I can say this with confidence to everyone reading this because of what God says in 1 Corinthians 2:9: *"What no eye has seen, what no ear has heard, and what no human mind has conceived" -- the things God has prepared for those who love him."*

When I think about my time at college, although those were some of the most exciting years of my life; I was also headed in the wrong direction. After being saved, I remember facing some of my old colleagues who were astonished by my transformation. They couldn't understand how God could take someone like me, a complete wreck, and change my life; there were times when I couldn't believe it myself.

You may be thinking: "what does any of this have to do with me finding a man?" A lot!

Your relationship with God and your transformation is the pillar of your foundation. It is what you stand on. That trip to State College was where I was able to let go of any disappointments I still harbored about my time and experiences while living and schooling in Pennsylvania and started a journey of complete healing from them.

Before any relationship, God wants to first be in a relationship with you. The world has done a great job of painting Him as a God who wants us to be bogged down in some ritualistic practices, traditions, or laws. The truth is that God the Father wants us as His sons and daughters. And just as God freely spoke these truths about State College, PA, being the place where the old me died, God wants to have conversations with you too.

God wants you to know that you are loved and valued by Him. He wants to be as intimate with you as you dream of being with your future husband. As you've dreamed about holding hands with your spouse and lying next to them while you both fall asleep to conversations that you don't want to end; God wants the same with you. He wants that level of intimacy and closeness. These are the key foundational values that we gain in our time of singleness.

"I will be a Father to you, and you will be my sons and daughters, says the Lord Almighty." (2 Corinthians 6:18)

One of the best decisions you will make in life, aside from who you choose to marry is accepting Jesus Christ as your Lord and Savior. God doesn't want to take any good from your life but rather rid you of what's bad and give you what is new! What grave clothes do you need to come out of? Is it the grave clothes of disappointment? Is it the grave clothes or rejection? Is it the grave clothes of sexual perversion?

Let it go!

REFLECTION

If you have gotten to this point in your life's journey and you are unsure of where you will spend eternity, and you are ready to accept God's love for you and allow Him to be the head of your life, then I want to say this repenter's prayer: *God, thank you for offering me the opportunity to spend eternity with you. I believe that you sent your Son Jesus to earth to die for my sins. I believe that He rose from the dead on the third day. I turn away from anything I've done that has placed a wedge between us. I thank you for your forgiveness and I open my heart now and I accept you as Lord of my life.*

> If you confess with your mouth that Jesus is Lord and believe in your heart that God raised him from the dead, you will be saved. (Romans 10:9)

If you've prayed this prayer for the first time, congratulations; your relationship with God has now begun!

If you have learned anything from reading this book, it's that repressing issues does not make them disappear. Being led by God, we should confront this situation head-on. Whether you have experienced abandonment from people or you feel disappointed by

God, your feelings matter. I want to encourage you to allow God the space to heal you. Give Him access to your heart and allow him to mend it back together.

LET'S PRAY

Heavenly Father, I come to you now because I need you. I need your help to heal this wounded heart. There have been times when I've hidden my feelings from you. I haven't always been real about them. Today, I let that go and I permit you to come in. I lay every weight of disappointment, dissatisfaction, and weariness down at your feet.

Thank you for never leaving me alone. You always find moments to remind me that you are with me. You said you'd never leave or forsake me, and I feel the truth in Your word. Now begin the mending, I am ready.

In Jesus' name. Amen

6.

Singleness is Not a Disease

When I am ready and have done all the necessary work on myself, the man will come. I used to believe this lie earlier in my singles journey! I am sure you have heard some version of these also:

> *"Get ready until he comes."*
>
> *"Work on yourself."*
>
> *"Learn to be submissive."*
>
> *"Go out more."*
>
> *"Be less aggressive."*

I surely have. And, in my desperate pursuit of marriage, I did everything I knew to do. I read the books on singleness and marriage, I watched the sermons and the YouTube videos on "the wait." I ran to the panel of married experts to see if maybe I missed a step in finding a husband. I was training myself to be a wife, and "working on myself" in preparation for marriage. I thought I needed to do more so that God would bring my mate. My life was consumed with "being the wife before the man comes." And it was the rhetoric every social media relationship "expert" was teaching.

I did the work. I was ready, but he still didn't show up. The man I thought I deserved after all this hard work was nowhere to be found. In frustration, I cried out, *"God, I've done everything! I read the books, I prepared, I watched the sermons, I worked on myself; EVERYTHING. Where is he?"*

And God said to me, "that's the problem, YOU did it! You never allowed ME to do it."

I cried my heart out after that revelation. It was a hard pill to swallow. I had no other choice but to surrender my will and my desire to get married to God. It was time for me to fall back and let God work. I needed the weight to fall off, it was too heavy for me.

I also learned a few valuable lessons from that intimate encounter with God, and those insights have changed my life and freed me up to live fully with or without a spouse.

Sis, regardless of what social media, reality TV, or society has shown us, singleness is not a disease. There is absolutely nothing wrong with being single and there is nothing wrong with us. We don't have to get ready or fix ourselves. As a single woman, I have had to constantly affirm this. It is not easy to lean into this truth, because the messages are everywhere. In every corner, there was a pastor or relationship expert teaching single women the steps they needed to take to get married or work on themselves to meet "the one."

I would listen while feeling a sense of inadequacy because I was doing everything "right." I had done all that I knew to do, and still, I remained single. This notion of working on ourselves without proper context will leave us thinking that we have the power to change ourselves, but that is not the case. Throughout the Bible, we find that narrative to be faulty. We read stories of *God* changing the hearts of people. It is God who changes us when we come to him. This truth is freedom, and it takes the shame and the pressure off.

It's hard to forget the shame that loomed over me when I'd sit in Bible study and the leader would constantly ask the single women, "what are you doing to prepare yourself for marriage?" My blood would boil in frustration as I left thinking, "I need to do more; I need to do more." It was deflating because the burden to prepare for marriage is often placed on single women. In many Christian spaces, women are often left with the brunt of having to prepare to be wives.

Society and the Church have influenced more women to jump into relationships than it has helped to embrace their singleness.

Men, on the other hand, are left with little to no expectations on how to prepare to be husbands. To make matters worse, there is a rise in male social media influencers who continue to perpetuate this toxic misogynistic view of black women. We are left with the expectations of being the only ones carrying the responsibilities in marriage while men are encouraged to place their attention and value on their network. *It be your own people sometimes.*

Furthermore, most of the marriage-focused books I've read, sermons I've listened to, and conferences I've attended, were aimed at single women. If preparation for men was mentioned, it was often in the small print. Many of my single girlfriends share this same grievance and frustration.

I'd often find this message of shame perpetuated among a lot of married women too. In conversations with married women, I found myself needing to clear my intentions for marriage. They questioned why I wanted to be married so badly. My desire to get married was not enough. I often felt like they were on a mountaintop talking down to me, the peasant in the valley, and that marriage to them was a secret society that only the elitist and privileged women get to be a part of. I felt small in comparison, and they felt untouchable and unrelatable.

These experiences were far from favorable. This type of shaming that places a burden on single women to "get right" and the man will come should never be our focus. However, I know that I wouldn't have written this book if those experiences were not part of my story. I am encouraging you to stop "working on yourself," especially "working on yourself to find a mate." Let God do the work through you! What does that look like? Turn your desires over to God! Spend time alone with God, and let Him know about your frustrations, your weariness, and your doubt. We are not sugarcoating our experiences and feelings; we are laying them on Jesus.

Don't get me wrong, we should always look to grow spiritually and prepare for our futures, but the burden to do so in hopes of marriage is not one God intends for us to carry. Don't spend your singleness solely preparing to be a wife. There is more to the future that God has for you.

That may be hard to hear, but Sis, I know what it feels like to remain single while everyone appears to be flourishing in relationships and marriages. I am with you, and we are living it together. I get weary of doing the "God" thing and seeing no results too. I get frustrated seeing all the engagement announcements and here I am still waiting on the one. Although I've experienced years of nothing but disappointment in relationships, I cannot idolize the idea of becoming a wife, and you shouldn't either.

When we think about idolatry from the Christian point of view, we picture someone offering sacrifices to a statue or an altar. However, not all idolatry appears to look like idolatry. God first mentions idolatry in the Ten commandments He gave to Moses after God delivered the Israelites from slavery in Egypt. These were the laws by which the Israelites were to abide.

One of the commandments was, *you shall have no other gods before me. You shall not make for yourself a carved image, or any likeness of anything that is in heaven above, or that is in the earth beneath, or that is in the water under the earth. You shall not bow down to them or serve them, for I the Lord your God am a jealous God, visiting the iniquity of the fathers on the children to the third and the fourth generation of those who hate me, but showing steadfast love to thousands of those who love me and keep my commandments. (Exodus 20:3-6.)*

The phrase "before me" indicates that we should not worship anything side by side or in conjunction with God. Benson's Commentary on Exodus 20 found on BibleHub.com, gives us great insight into how we can turn our desires into gods. *"Pride makes a god of ourselves, covetousness makes a god of money, sensuality makes a god of the belly. Whatever is loved, feared, delighted in, or depended on, more than God, that we make a god of."*

I had made my desire for marriage an idol so much that it had become my focus over my purpose and my relationship with God. Before we are to marry our husbands, we are to marry Christ, and our love for our future husbands should never outweigh our love for God. The danger in idolizing a thing is that you don't always see how that thing takes precedence over God, but it does. Idolizing marriage leads to fascination and eventually empty promises and further disappointments.

REFLECTION

Singleness is painted as some deadly disease that needs to be cured, mostly among women. Everywhere single women turn, some marketing scheme insists we are faulty because we are unmarried. The exact opposite is true. Singleness is a time for God to work on our hearts and prepare us for marriage.

It's also a time to explore, travel, and meet new people. Simply speaking, singleness is a grace period that allows us to "get busy" doing the Lord's work. Don't get so caught up in this rush to find a mate. Relax your shoulders a bit. I know being single and dating, can be 'ghetto' sometimes, but dragging your feet for your single years won't bring you peace or reveal purpose.

If I were to be married years ago, I wouldn't have experienced so much life, so much freedom. Take heart girl, in the right time, God will align you with the purpose mate He has promised.

LET'S PRAY

Dear God, thank you for placing the desire to be married in my heart. I give you permission, even now to remove any misconceptions that I have about what marriage looks like to you.

Help me to understand what the covenant of marriage is in your eyes and prepare me for my future mate. Help me to keep my eyes and hands on the work that you have called me to do in my single season.

Do not let idolatry keep me from what you have for me. I thank you for the purposes you've given me, and I declare that I will not leave my work undone.

In Jesus' name. Amen.

7.

Be Free from Concern

Paul, the author of 1st and 2nd Corinthians, penned a letter to a group of believers in the church of Corinth who were rejecting God's way of living. In that letter, I think Paul did a great job of explaining what our single season is to be used for and what we should focus on.

He says: *"**I would like you to be free from concern**. An unmarried man is concerned about the Lord's affairs—how he can please the Lord. But a married man is concerned about the affairs of this world—how he can please his wife— and his interests are divided. An unmarried woman or virgin is concerned about the Lord's affairs: **Her aim is to be devoted** to the Lord **in both body and spirit**. But a married woman is concerned about the affairs of this world—how she can please her husband. **I am saying this for your own good, not to restrict you**, but that you may live in a right way in undivided devotion to the Lord."*

It took me a long time to process this scripture, but eventually, I understood why Paul encouraged us with this message. I have always been drawn to the sentence; **I would like you to be free from concern**. It is an affirming statement that indicates that God does not beat us over the head with rules and regulations. Instead, He encourages, warns, directs, and corrects us **for our good**. He offers us freedom and a life free of worry.

Paul also encourages us to give our undivided **attention** to God and to be of service to Him and others, while we are single. When our attention is committed to God, it helps take to the focus off of our relationship status and onto God. Paul drives this point home by providing us with insight into how single life differs from married life. Although Paul desired that all would be single like him, he realized that everyone did not have the gift of abstinence.

While celibacy and abstinence have become interchangeable words in contemporary society, celibacy is a choice to live without sex forever, abstinence is not. Celibacy is what is practiced by Catholic Priests through a vow of celibacy. When I mention celibacy in this book, however, note that I am not referencing a lifetime vow to never have sex. Paul recognized that everyone did not have the gift or desire to do so and with this, he said it is better to wed.

While it is better for one to marry than to be consumed with sexual desires, according to Paul, his discourse stresses how important it is to be single also. Being single is an opportunity to get to the heart of what God wants you to address; your purpose, your identity, and an intimate relationship with God are all things to explore in your singleness. I've felt that so much importance is placed on marriage and none on singleness.

The idea of having a "better-half" is a worldly perspective that has snuck its way into the church. And although not always verbalized, this perspective appears to be held by many married believers. I believe this is mostly because Christians see marriage as a symbol of true wholeness. Being unmarried means you are *clearly* missing something.

This is probably why so much importance is placed on marriage. Now, reading this book, you will come to understand that I strongly desire marriage. Although I have a desire for marriage, I recognize how important my single season is when considering the bigger picture. Our singleness is a period of grace that God allows us, it's not a sickness, there's nothing wrong with you, and you are not missing your "other half." You will, if you allow God to do the work in you, become whole in Him before you meet your spouse. Your time of singleness is not only important but necessary.

I am sure God has given you dreams and laid projects on your heart. He may even have called you to go places. Don't miss out on your opportunity by focusing so much on when your man is going to come, not when there is so much more that God has called you to do. Let's use our time of singleness to uncover purposes, solidify our identity, and make our faith in Him complete. God has all of this available for you in your singleness. He wants to make you whole and complete, in Him, lacking nothing.

I say this because I understand how much of a distraction singleness can be. Some of you reading this are stuck because your perspective on singleness has kept you stagnant. You're *just 'waiting' on a husband.* There's too much purpose in you for you to sit still simply waiting to be found. Let's take the story of the first man, Adam, into consideration. He was single before Eve was formed.

In Adam's singleness, the Bible mentioned that God tasked him with naming the animals. I picture Adam going around the garden using his creativity to think up a name for each animal. What an amazing task God entrusted to Adam. Sis, there are things God has tasked you to do and even more that he wants to entrust to you. Remember that if God gave you a desire to get married, then this season of waiting, like all others, is temporary.

Here are some more scriptures to reflect on:

"And don't be wishing you were someplace else or with someone else. Where you are right now is God's place for you. Live and obey, love, and believe right there. God, not your marital status, defines your life. Don't think I'm being harder on you than on the others. I give this same counsel in all the churches." (1 Corinthians 7:17 MSG)

And,

> " I want you to live as free of complications as possible. When you're unmarried, you're free to concentrate on **simply pleasing the Master**. Marriage involves you in all the nuts and bolts of domestic life and in wanting to please your spouse, leading to so many more demands on your attention. The time and energy that married people spend on caring for and nurturing each other, the unmarried can spend in **becoming whole and holy instruments of God**."
> (1 Corinthians: 7: 32-35 MSG)

If we look at our journey to marriage as a faith walk, then James 1:3-4 can apply.

> "For you know that when your faith is tested, your endurance has a chance to grow. So let it grow, for when your endurance is fully developed, you

will be perfect and complete, needing nothing."

Consider this; when you are married, you will be consumed with your husband and family. But while you are single, you are free. In our freedom, we are to fill our time with serving God's people, building intimacy with God, allowing God to heal us, producing endurance, and walking towards our earthly purposes. So, let's worship God and move marriage off the altar before it becomes an idol.

REFLECTION

If you are not clear on your identity or purpose, that's quite okay; you are in the perfect position to discover this. This is a season of discovery and healing.

The journey to discovering yourself starts with a desire but takes time and much patience. Uncovering the wounds from trauma, discovering our identity, and walking out your purpose is not a pain-free experience, but one that is necessary and only accomplished if we let God nurture us.

Just like a tree, when the time is right - the soil has been dug, debris cleared out, and the seeds planted - you will sprout from the ground with strong roots to grow.

I must speak these truths to you: The man that God has for you *will* pick you. You won't have to chase after him, lose your morals to get him, or lose yourself to keep Him! Let God do a complete work inside of you so that you can have a marriage that lasts in a society that has a 50% divorce rate.

Use this season to discover your purpose and God will reveal when you take some time today to pray and seek him out.

Pay attention to what He tells you.

After you've spent some time with God in your spiritual mirror, look at a few ways God intends for us to be:

1. Be Wise – Proverbs 4:6-7

2. Be Loving – Luke 6:35

3. Be Kind – Ephesians 4:32

4. Be Faithful – Deuteronomy 5:32-33

5. Be Humble – Romans 12:16

6. Be Patient – Psalm 27:14

7. Be Joyous – John 16:22

8. Be Willing – Isaiah 1:19

9. Be Giving – Deuteronomy 15:10

10. Be Strong – Ephesians 6:10

Then reflect on and answer these questions:

- Apart from waiting on marriage, how do you plan on becoming the woman that God has created you to be?
- What are you going to do in your singleness that will prepare you for your future whether marriage is in the picture or not?
- Are you ready to go at this alone?

LET'S PRAY

Dear God, thank you for placing the desire to be married in my heart. I give you permission, even now to remove any misconceptions that I have about what marriage looks like to you.

Help me to understand what the covenant of marriage is in your eyes and prepare me for my future mate. Help me to keep my eyes and hands on the work that you have called me to do in my single season.

Do not let idolatry keep me from what you have for me. I thank you for the purposes you've given me, and I declare that I will not leave my work undone.

In Jesus' name. Amen.

8.

The Weight of the Wait

I was "ready and prepared (set)" for marriage according to the world's standards, but what I soon realized was that the world's standards and our timing seldom line up with God's timing and God's terms. We believe that once we have everything in order - reached the right age, worked on ourselves, sought out counsel, prayed, fasted, etc. - that God will send us the man. WAIT is the most unlikely term we expect to hear after we're READY and SET. It is simply not the natural order of things.

However, when I decided to journey with God, I soon realized that I'd been given misinformation about this whole dating thing for years. It took me a year to finally pick up my pen and finish this chapter because God needed me to understand what the "waiting" part looked like after being ready and set.

One of the hardest things I've had to do is to share and encourage from a place of my struggles.

As I pen these words to you, it is an encouragement to me too. Our waiting is not in vain, but it can be hard to see it when we can't see it! Years ago, I decided to become abstinent (I share more about my abstinence journey in an upcoming chapter). Honestly, the first two years were a breeze. It's the last six or so years after that have been the hardest. After losing my dad, it seemed as though the struggle intensified. The feeling of abandonment and rejection coupled themselves with loneliness and grief, but I found respite in Galatians 6:9.

> "And let us not be weary in well doing:
> for in due season we shall reap if we faint
> not."

This scripture helped me to put how I was feeling into words and in context – weary. I was weary! The word weary still pops off the pages of the Bible whenever I read it. I was weary, disappointed, and discouraged. I still have moments when my season of singleness felt like it would have no end. I remember praying so fervently to God, asking Him to remove the desire for marriage if it wasn't in His plans for me. I had to pray about this because it was hurting me to believe and trust that God had someone for me. I was tired of being single and I was tired of being abstinent. Heck, I was tired of being tired.

Interestingly, God encourages us to "not be weary in well-doing." Is it because He knew that doing the right thing would be HARD? I certainly believe so. There have been countless moments when I've questioned God about His promise to me for marriage. I've asked Him many times: "What is the use of waiting"?

I've felt weary to the point of exhaustion. I've wanted to and have given up so many times. I've been angry, disappointed, and envious of what others have. I've poured my tears and words out onto the pages of my journals and in the ears of my friends. I had a really hard time sharing the raw frustrations of this wait with others because of shame. There were so many days when I wanted to hide. I didn't want the world to know that I was still waiting with no prospects in sight while I encouraged others. The year 2020 amplified the weight of the wait for so many of us.

While a widespread pandemic threatened the health and safety of the entire world, it also threatened our freedom. There were talks of shutdowns looming, and I had just moved into my first apartment. COVID, as we all knew it, challenged us all in so many different ways. Single mothers were concerned about how they would maintain their employment while having to homeschool, their children, adult children worried about the safety of their at-risk senior parents, and single women worried about how they would find love behind closed doors and masked faces. I was one of those women.

I didn't know how I would respond to truly being alone. If you've read *The Five Love Languages: How to Express Heartfelt Commitment to Your Mate Book* by Gary Chapman, you've probably determined what your love language is.

Although not biblical, it is a good reference/resource for discovering how you receive love. Of the five love languages discussed in Chapman's book, my top two are acts of service and quality time. Not being able to spend quality time with those I loved, made me feel unloved. That, coupled with my singleness, made me feel unwanted. However, what felt like being closed off from the world was actually a divine appointment for me to develop a deeper relationship with God. I needed to drown out the world's standards and noise and align my life and desires with God's timing and God's terms. I drowned out the noise through worship songs, devotional time, and journaling with God.

For weeks, I was able to block out the noise of the world, the opinions of others, my thoughts, and my fear, and replace it with a singular focus on God. Sometimes, surviving the weariness and weight of singleness meant crying out to God and laying before him (literally laying on the floor of my apartment and expressing my grievances). I'd encourage you to pick whatever tools work for you and when it stops working find something new. Don't beat yourself up because you feel lonely. The hope is that we will not lose hope on our journey to marriage. The reality is that sometimes we will. We will feel weary, and the charge is to lean in Christ.

Although spending time with God is not a popular concept in mainstream media and culture, it is essential. The coronavirus pandemic proved to the world how much we truly need God. My time during lockdown reminded me of God's purpose for me and His purpose for all of humanity. It helped me to let go of my fears and concerns about my singleness by surrendering my life to God and shifting my focus. I was able to identify and acknowledge God's truths concerning my life versus the enemy's lies and the world's standards.

The lockdown during the pandemic was a condensed version of my years of waiting, but the best thing I did for myself during the lockdown was "getting real" with myself and with the weariness I felt. There were many days when all I was left with were my tears and emotions. Saying "I am angry" turned into: "I'm disappointed," "I feel let down," "I feel left behind," and "I feel rejected." Sometimes, seeing what others had made me feel like I was missing out on something. I felt like God had completely forgotten about me. I would compare where I was to others and then ask God why my life didn't look like theirs.

This covetousness and jealousy only made me bitter towards God. Through my time in quarantine, I was able not only to identify these feelings but to allow God to work on my heart. If there's one thing I will continue to encourage you to do, it's this: identify how you really feel. As women, we need to stop taking on the notion that we always have to be strong! We need to take off the masks called "Yes, I'm fine" and "I'll be okay," and get real, raw, and vulnerable with our emotions. We need to trust God and walk by faith – as small as it may be.

Vulnerable faith.

Raw faith.

Crazy faith.

Real faith.

Unadulterated faith.

"God-I-don't-know-how-you're-going-to-do-it-but-I-pray-you-do-it" faith.

Give the weight to God. Don't let the weight of the weight cause you to sin. Stand on God's promises – and wait on His very best.

"Wherefore, seeing we also are compassed about with so great a cloud of witnesses, let us lay aside every weight, and the sin which doth so easily beset us, and let us run with patience the race that is set before us. (Hebrews 12:1)

REFLECTION

For some, the 2020 pandemic brought love. For others like me, it was marked by loneliness in the beginning. Then somewhere along the way, as I began to explore my relationship with God more deeply, what turned out to be the worst of times was actually very stretching and intimate.

If the pandemic didn't leave you feeling even more discouraged about your singleness, maybe it was something else. Maybe you had a season where you felt like you would be single forever. Perhaps this is the way you feel currently. If this is the case, I want to encourage you to explore your relationship with God.

How can you spend intentional time with Him? Lay at the Lord's feet. Let your burdens fall off your shoulders and at the feet of God. You do this by being honest about how you feel and spending intentional quality time with God.

LET'S PRAY

Dear God, time has revealed how much I truly need you. There is no way that I can walk through my singleness season without your grace and your strength. Thank you, Lord, that you do not leave us alone. Thank you for leaving the pack to attend to me. You are El Roi, the God who sees me. With you, I am never alone or without. You comfort me in my times of weariness, and you fill me in my times of despair! Thank you. My prayer is that you will continue to empower me in my single season to trust you. Help me to continually surrender my will and my timeline to you. As I wait, continue to download visions and dreams in me and give me the resources required to carry them out to completion. When my mate comes, I will be ready because you have taken your time to prepare me for him.

In Jesus' name. Amen.

9.

Heading in the Wrong Direction

Towards the end of the pandemic, I was ready to come out of hiding and get back onto the dating scene. It was the start of *#hotgirlsummer* and I was trying to stay as holy as possible, but I also wanted to dress up, get pretty, and enjoy some quality time with a nice gentleman.

Ironically, before going out on a date with Trevor, I told a friend that I'd become tired of dudes tiptoeing around asking me out in my DMs. "So, do you want him to be forceful and aggressive?" she asked. In typical New York fashion, I said, "Yes, I want him to get to the point, do you want to marry me or not?"

I wasn't a hundred percent serious about the marriage part, but I did desire a more aggressive approach from men. I was tired of trying to guess my way through dates – were they interested in me or not? Be careful what you pray for because God is listening.

Less than a week later, I got a DM from Trevor. We had met a few summers before this interaction.

Trevor complimented me on my looks and asked me where I lived. He then proceeded to say, and I quote: "I'm in your area, get dressed and I will pick you up at 8."

Can I be honest? I was open.

I was willing to risk it all for this 8 p.m. meetup, but I had to take a minute to analyze what was happening. This was a stranger who "happened to be" in my area and wanted to have an impromptu date. All the relationship "expert" advice I had heard and read throughout my singleness journey, suddenly began ringing in my ears. "Be open, be flexible, be willing, show him you're interested." I decided, instead, to go with my gut and responded, "I'm not free tonight, but would love to meet for lunch during the week."

Trevor and I then made plans to meet in his hometown the following week. "I'm in your area, get dressed" turned into "let's meet in my hometown."

I must be honest with myself and say, I skipped this red flag in our planning for this date. It was as if everything was centered around his convenience. Some of you reading this may feel that this is an opinion based on preference, however, this was a red flag to me. Others may think I'm foolish for entertaining the idea of traveling this far to meet for a first date. I toyed with both perspectives, ignored the red flag, and hopped on a train to meet Trevor in his hometown. Yes, I was on a train to meet this stranger in his hometown.

I was hit in the face with the second red flag when Trevor was late meeting me at the train station. I understand that "things happen," however it was completely irresponsible of him to be thirty minutes late without giving me a heads up. At this point, I didn't expect much from Trevor.

I was right not to because Trevor and I proved to be clearly incompatible in our faith and perspective on a lot of things. The first question he asked me when we met was, "so do you have a ratchet side?" *What? What does that even mean?* I thought. He then went on to tell me about his experiences with black women. They have been aggressive, he said. *Too* independent, confrontational, and unwilling to submit. I just sat and listened, mostly because I've learned to say less and listen more during dates. You'll be surprised what you learn about the person when you just listen and let them talk. His misogynistic and toxic views of black women didn't stop there. As the date progressed, he went on to say:

- Black women should just be quiet, docile, and submissive because Black men can find non-black immigrant women to marry instead of them. Yes, he said this.

- He also used the bible to express his belief that a woman's role was to leave her passion, purposes, and God-given dreams to follow the vision of her husband. "There's no such thing as a wife saying God told me to do this," he said to further his point about a woman's role to submit to her husband.

- When speaking about traumatic childhood experiences that often plague black women, he offered up no grace and expressed a complete lack of empathy.

- He also mentioned that it was a woman's role to shut up in the church and let the man lead and speak.

He continued with his anti-black woman rhetoric which was very resemblant to that of one popular internet relationship expert. I listened and took notes because, at this point, my dating experiences had become content for this book.

That conversation is a clear example of why it is important to explore and recognize misalignment in core values and beliefs. I learned from this situation never to ignore the red flags because of desperation. Listen, I get it. I want to be married just like the next person but settling is a long-term commitment.

At first, it seems okay, but have you met people in relationships with people they settled with? I'm not talking about looks! What about your purpose?

If I had settled for Trevor, I would have been sacrificing the promises God made to me. I was not created to be this quiet, in-the-background person, and I completely accept and love that about myself. I am no longer willing to hang my gifts up on a shelf to be in a relationship and neither should you. Do you believe that the man God has for you will complement you? You should. I believe that my God-ordained spouse will not only draw me closer to God but will pull more purpose out of me. I am bold enough to believe that our purposes will align. We will be each other's helpmates. Can I challenge you to believe the same?

Although Trevor was a tall, decent-looking, Christian man, who checked off all the "equally yoked" boxes on paper, we weren't equally yoked.

Unfortunately, scripture included in a man's bio, or even his verbal profession of faith, cannot be used as a determination of being equally yoked. Thinking "He's a Christian and I'm a Christian," is not enough to determine whether or not you two are compatible in your faith. Do you carry the same core beliefs and values when it comes to salvation? Does he believe one can lose their salvation and you believe that "once saved always saved?" Does he believe you are saved by grace and you believe we are saved by works? What are his views on submission? Does he believe that a woman should stay quiet in the church? Do you carry the same beliefs? These are only some things to consider when we are determining who we are and are not equally yoked with.

Trevor wasn't the first man to almost have me heading in the wrong direction. There was also Brian.

Brian and I met on a dating app. Strangely enough, we were *destined* to meet. At least, that's what I thought! Please don't laugh at me, but I didn't know then that Tinder was for hooking up only. Where had I been?

"I met a guy I am really digging," I said to a close friend of mine. When I described him to her, she responded with excitement; "that's the guy who acted in the play I invited you to." True to who I used to be, I took that as a sign that he and I were destined to meet. You see, earlier on in my dating season, I listened to my share of YouTube videos on dating and read tons of books. I'd become my own relationship expert by virtue of the information I consumed.

A consistent thread in the kingdom marriage testimonies I'd heard was, "I knew he was the one, because...," and this was a trap I fell into often in my dating experiences. Instead of bringing a new connection to God in prayer, I'd ignore any and all red flags while leaning into flimsy "signs" that indicated he was the one for me. I idolized the idea of marriage, and my desire was overwhelming and consuming. I focused so much on the end goal, that I consistently bypassed the obvious signs that Brian and I were not equally yoked or compatible.

If you have been in church for any amount of time, you may have heard the phrase "unequally yoked." What does this mean and how can we apply it to our lives? A yoke is an instrument often a wooden beam used to bind the heads of two animals together. The goal is to pair together oxen or other animals **to enable them to pull on a load in the same direction at the same time.**

> "**Be ye not unequally yoked together with unbelievers**, for what fellowship hath righteousness with unrighteousness? and what communion hath light with darkness?" (2 Corinthians 6:14)

Apostle Paul was warning the church of Corinth against being joined together in partnerships with unbelievers. Some have argued that Paul is not speaking about marriage because he made no mention of it in this chapter, however, he is referencing relationships, and a marriage is a relationship.

Others have argued that we should "do away" with religions like Christianity because of the rules. However, it is important to note that Christianity is a faith relationship, and we must get into the heart of what Paul is teaching the Corinthians in this particular verse.

Primarily, we made Christianity into a religion. When we look at Jesus' life and teachings, He was fiercely against religion. He fought against religion, religious leaders, rules, and laws, during his entire ministry. It is important to highlight this because it leads us to the essence of why what Paul is warning us against is not a "religious rule" but a different perspective and way to engage in relationships.

Paul is not teaching that Christians and Muslims can't be friends or that Christians and Buddhists cannot commune together. What he is saying is, make sure you know who you are joining together with so that you *know* what direction you two are headed in. When two oxen or animals are bound together with a yoke, the goal is to go in the same direction. It would be impossible for a farmer to get his field plowed if one ox decides to go left and the other goes straight. The workday will be very long.

Before I get back to Brian, let's ground this concept into our everyday lives. When I was working as a retail manager, I needed to take Sundays off because I attended church. The company I worked for was not founded on Christian values. In fact, they did not allow managers to have weekends off. By the grace of God, I was able to take Sundays off, but only because I fought my case and stood by my convictions. It was not easy; there were days when I almost backed down and worked, but I stood with God, and He made a way for me.

I just worked for this company but imagine if this company were a man I was dating. Imagine having to fight my case to attend Church every Sunday. Imagine that we did not share the same values or convictions on serving God's people, and every time I needed to answer a call to pray for someone who was in desperate need of help, he complained because he didn't have the same convictions.

Now, imagine being married to this person whom you are to honor as the head of the home. Would you find yourself still fighting to keep your convictions or would you just head in his direction and give them up? This is what Paul is talking about. Unbelievers are not just those who don't share the same faith as us, but also those who don't have the same convictions and beliefs. Do not be unequally yoked, do not be with someone who does not share the same morals as you.

With that caution and insight from Paul at the back of our minds, let's jump back into my alliances with Brian. As I said earlier, we were not equally yoked and neither were we compatible, but true to the resounding theme of my earlier years as a single woman, the soundtrack remained. I desperately wanted love. I desperately wanted to be married. I desperately wanted my single season to end... So I ignored the red flags and leaned into all the signs that said we were meant to be. Signs like, he was my *type*, he was creative, and he was a believer. Everything seemed to line up, and that's all I thought I needed. So I overlooked the basics.

He wasn't ready for a commitment because he hadn't been fully healed. Above all, he wasn't actively pursuing me. Yes, he was a believer, but he would often mock me about my relationship with God. His words about my convictions were not at all reassuring. I'd developed a very intimate relationship with God at the time I met Brian. It was a relationship I had never experienced before. I was super passionate about sharing God's word with everyone, but I was also a bit ashamed. I remember feeling corny for being a Christian. I didn't see many people my age serving God. Unfortunately, I didn't have a community of like-minded friends back then and his harmful words affected my self-confidence. My desire to be accepted, loved, and married, superseded my discernment so I ignored all the red flags.

Instead of leaning into the caution in **Amos 3:3,** *"Do two walk together unless they have agreed to do so?"*

Another version says, *"Can two people walk together without agreeing on the direction?"*

I decided to help him walk with me. I spent my days counseling him, trying to help push him closer to God in an attempt to selfishly make him the man for me. I was less concerned about his soul and more concerned about molding him into the husband I so desperately wanted him to be. I fooled myself into thinking that it was what I was supposed to do. Aren't we supposed to *make them better men*? I consistently showed up, was always available, and desperately craved his time and attention.

What did *he* do? He became what I *wanted* when I *wanted it*. He would listen to my cues, and my desire for marriage, and he would play off of them. Through the inconsistencies, he still managed to say all the right things. I was disillusioned. His actions rarely lined up with his words. He would speak of *our* future together and paint these beautiful pictures of what life would look like. When describing what he wanted in a wife, he would mention all of my characteristics without mentioning my name. He wanted my attention and emotions with no plans of being truly committed to me.

This disillusionment eventually led me down a path of disappointment. He would throw words and scenarios at me and wait for me to catch them. And because his actions and his words never lined up, he left me chasing after who I thought he was. I was running after who I wanted him to be while he left me a trail of crumbs.

I not only made marriage an idol in my heart, but I made Brian an idol as well. He was never the man God had for me, but I was blinded by my desires. I don't remember bringing him to God or asking God what He thought about my connection with Him. God says He knows the heart of man; hence we can be certain that God knows the best person for us.

> "But the Lord said to Samuel, "Do not look at his appearance or at his physical stature, because I have refused him. For the Lord does not see as man sees; for man looks at the outward appearance, but the Lord looks at the heart." (1 Samuel 16:7 NKJV).

We look at what we physically see, but it is God who knows the heart and the motives of man. He knew this man's motives were wrong, it was not because he was a bad person, but he wasn't healed nor was he ready for love.

The unfortunate thing about my experience with Brian is that what happened with him is common. I speak to so many women who have been led down this path of disappointment, just as I was. We stay in situationships with men with the hopes that one day they will choose us. "Maybe one day we will be good enough," we think. I'm sure there is a face of a man you are seeing in your mind as you read this right now. I want you to know that you are not alone.

Whenever a woman asks me how she can determine whether the guy she is dating or interested in is the right one, I encourage her to consider whether she has peace with it.

Here's the thing about Brian, he was a counterfeit, and I was not completely blindsided by him, my desires simply overtook me. I saw the red flags! In his case, the counterfeit was pretty obvious. What about when it's not and you are struggling to determine if a man is the right one to keep walking with?

Well, let's examine a counterfeit dollar bill. If it's your first time seeing one, you may be easily deceived into thinking it's real. BUT after having encountered it a few times, you are more easily able to spot it. Brian was already running from commitment to his own personal endeavors. He would start a project and never finish it, he would make plans and "forget," he would speak about past relationships with an unhealed heart, and he was always moving. He wasn't ready for marriage nor was he the man that God had for me. He was easy to spot.

I have never made counterfeit money before, but I can imagine that in order to produce a counterfeit dollar bill, you must study the characteristics of the real thing in order to mimic it. This is what my experience was when dating and dealing with counterfeit men. Remember, a man God sends will walk in the same direction as you.

Anytime I have found myself shrinking back or hiding my full identity while dating, it has been a clear indication that the relationship was a counterfeit and not for me. I believe that God has created us all with individual and very unique purposes to advance His Kingdom (God's message of Salvation).

Our purposes are all manifested in different ways. If we look at the fact that we are all created to spread the Gospel of God's love, then what are our future spouses called to do? The same. If we meet a man who is not in alignment with God's purpose and as a result does not accept yours, then he is not the one for you; sadly, he is a counterfeit. I must caution you.

Even as I am explaining what a counterfeit is, you must seek God for direction on your own. Bring every connection and relationship to God in prayer and ask Him for clarity in recognizing counterfeits! If we think about counterfeit money, as time has passed, it has gotten more deceptive. Do not be deceived by a counterfeit appearing real. I hope that in sharing my experience with Brian, you start to look at counterfeits from the right lens and avoid a lot of the disappointments I had to endure.

This is a question that I want to leave up to you to answer. Before you go any further, ask yourself this question. Maybe it's someone you're currently dating; can you walk together without agreeing on the direction? Are you two headed in the same direction? Can you stand to walk in the direction he is leading you? Would you be okay being yoked together with this individual?

Maybe you aren't dating yet, great, this is your time to explore your convictions. This is the time that God is giving you to uncover your identity and to know who you are in Him. You will have all of these values + convictions to bring to the table when it's your time to wed. God loves us so much that He gave us His Word so that in following it, we would avoid a lot of the consequences, burdens, and disappointments of life.

For me, being equally yoked in relationships means that I cannot afford to date a man who doesn't have a heart for God, God's community, and God's people, and doesn't love and stand by God's word. Although, I knew and know this; my desperation and loneliness have led me to date a lot of counterfeits. I would often say: "I can write a book on counterfeits" because I've had so many experiences with counterfeit men.

These experiences led to countless disappointments that made me feel as if I would never get married. These counterfeit relationships were strategically placed to distract me and derail me from God's best. If you are dating someone not sent from God, then who sent him?

REFLECTION

Singleness is a journey. On this journey, you will have many roads to take. The key to navigating our singleness is to let God lead the way. Sometimes we don't. I've found myself headed in the wrong direction with my share of counterfeits.

Sometimes I was able to dodge the bullet unscathed but other times, it left me with a wound that would take time to heal. I would like to encourage you to trust your discernment and look at the signs. It will be very apparent if the man before you is for you or not.

You may feel that knot in your stomach that says, something isn't quite right. Maybe you are blatantly seeing all the red flags. This ain't a carnival,

Sis, don't ignore the signs. Trust what you are seeing and feeling and don't be duped by a counterfeit. God wants the best for you and so do I.

LET'S PRAY

Dear heavenly Father, I thank you for the gift of discernment. Help me to stop ignoring the signs and trust the red flags when I see and feel them. Help me to be strong enough to walk away from relationships or the possibility of a relationship that will not serve me or my purpose. Help me to endure until my purpose mate comes.

Thank you for this gentle reminder that you want what's best for me. Thank you for being so intentional with me. Your word says that you watch over your word to perform. If you promised me a mate, you will attend to the promise to ensure it is brought to its full manifestation. I thank you, and today I commit to honoring myself by waiting on your very best.

In Jesus' name. Amen.

10.

Unmasking The Mystery Man

I had a bad habit; one I believe many single women have. It is a habit that has gotten us into relationships and situationships with men we know are not good for us. They are counterfeits waving red flags at every turn, but still, we push forward, or they are God-fearing men who are not ready, but yet we push forward.

It is the bad habit of creating a bunch of "fairy tale imaginations and what-ifs" about a man we barely know. I have found myself daydreaming about a man and picturing what life would be like with him if things worked out between us. I'd plan our life together in my head before giving the man a chance to show me his true self. Sometimes, even after revealing his true self, I would press on.

My desperation was a magnet that attracted counterfeits. Men would show up and become who I wanted them to be only to turn around and drain me of my time and energy. I'd given so many men space in my life, heart, and spirit. The imaginations and "what-ifs" opened doors in my spirit to allow the enemy to tempt me with what I thought I wanted, and it only led to more rejection and abandonment.

For the past few years of my abstinence journey, around the same time every year, I would get the same feeling of depression. As soon as November rolled around, what started as grief would quickly turn into extreme loneliness. Simultaneously, my Instagram feed was filled with engagements, family photos, and baby announcements. I was reminded that it was another year of singleness and no husband in sight. For years, I kept these feelings to myself out of sheer humiliation and embarrassment. I felt so alone in my thoughts and wondered how I would be viewed for my feelings. Loneliness can be such an isolating and humiliating experience.

We have all been down Lonely Street before; it's on the corner of I Should Call My Ex Lane and right next to that STOP sign. We say to God: "God, please show me a sign that he isn't the right one for me. God screams: "SIGN" and we put our headphones in. We don't want to hear the truth because we are lonely and tired of being lonely. Sometimes, we'd rather settle into a relationship to end the loneliness than wait on God's best. Let me say that again, sometimes, we'd rather settle into a relationship to end the loneliness than wait on God's best.

Loneliness is a heart condition that only God can cure. There are people in relationships right now who are still lonely. Do not be disillusioned. Loneliness opens a door that invites the devil right in and we are blinded to the counterfeits and the red flags. When I experienced loneliness, it didn't come by itself but brought its friends: vulnerability, weariness, and desperation. Sometimes we get so lonely that we open the door to men we should have kept on the other side of the door.

Let's look at what God says about loneliness in Isaiah 41:10 (NIV):

> So do not fear, for I am with you; do not
> be dismayed, for I am your God. I will
> strengthen you and help you; I will
> uphold you with my righteous right
> hand.

For I am with you! We can pull that word out of this text and understand that God, Our Father in Heaven is with us on earth. He is not a big figment of our imagination. He is with us. God walks alongside us and desires to commune with us. In our singleness, we can develop a level of intimacy that is necessary for every relationship. Your relationship with God is monumental and will become the building block upon which you build your marriage.

Do not run away from your alone time with God, and do not rush into marriage out of fear of loneliness; allow yourself to become one with God.

I remember another season when I was so desperate for marriage, that the loneliness led me to another counterfeit who was dripping red flags. It was the beginning of a particularly low season in my life. The retail store where I'd been working was closing, and I was to soon become unemployed.

One day, a fine gentleman walked into the store and immediately caught my eye. When he approached the cash register, we sparked a conversation in which he overtly flirted with me. I stepped to the side after the transaction, and we exchanged numbers. Before we exchanged numbers, I perceived something quite mysterious and dark in his eyes. It was jeering. "There is something mysterious about you," I blurted out. "I can't figure it out, but I see it." He assured me that I was imagining things.

Later that evening, we had our first phone conversation. Within the first few minutes of speaking, we got to the topic of faith and I expressed to him my faith as a Christian. Then I proceeded to talk about my journey with God. Every word that came out of my mouth from that point on was mimicked by him.

"So you go to church?" he asked.

"Yes," I replied.

"Me too," he said.

"So, do you drink?" he asked.

"Only wine, on occasion," I said.

"Oh, same here," he uttered.

"What type of music do you listen to?" he asked.

"I only *really* listen to gospel," I said.

"Oh yeah, me too," he exclaimed.

He continued to pick my brain about my favorite gospel artists and had lots of questions and a lot of similar responses. This was a huge red flag for me but it did not stop me from having conversations with him. In that same conversation, he began to say things that reminded me of the characteristics I'd prayed for in my husband. There was one particular statement he made that made me certain that God had sent him.

After hours of conversation, we concluded our call and I was left with my thoughts. I took out my list of qualities I wanted in a husband and began to cross off every line he checked. As I was going down the list, I began to cry because he checked off every mark.

That night, I prayed to God: "God, I hope He is the one, but if he is not, please show me."

We went on a few dates, and he was putting his best foot forward. I assumed that he was into me. Our phone calls and facetime conversations would go into the wee hours of the morning. We talked frequently (every single day). He would wake me up in the morning with scriptures and devotionals, he was becoming who he thought I wanted him to be.

While we were getting to know each other, I had mentioned to him that I was searching for a new job and he was helping me to find work. Remember, the store where I was working was closing and I was going to be unemployed.

He said he knew someone who could help and offered me an "amazing opportunity" with one of his "friends." He connected me with her and set up the interview, and even helped prepare me for the interview. He also read over my resume and gave me tips.

Then the story began to take a very weird turn. What appeared to be a kind gesture, something aligned with the type of man I desired, turned out to be a deceptive strategy.

On that particular day when the story shifted, I had begun to feel anxious about him for some reason. My spirit was so unsettled. I had gone for the interview a few days prior and noticed that his texts and morning check-ins had almost immediately ceased.

I was on the sales floor that day when I left to go and sit in the office to get my thoughts together. As I sat there, I felt my heart racing, so I began to pray.

"God, please show me the truth about this man," I whispered to God. Then I heard God speak very clearly.

"Text him right now about the job opportunity, if he responds *immediately,* I will reveal to you the motive."

I picked up my phone and texted something random about the job opportunity. Mind you, I had not heard from him all day. After I sent him the text, I quickly turned my phone over to ease the anxiety of the moment. He texted me right back.

Then God said, "it was never about you. He was schmoozing for the job; he is a recruiter."

I don't know what told him I was on to him after that text, but he started to respond with a lot of questions back-to-back. Then he started begging to call and speak to me, but I didn't respond. I waited until the following day to talk to him because as you can imagine, I was disappointed that he had deceived me. I sent him a text ending things. I expressed that including ending all communication with him, I would not be taking the job.

He pretended to be who I wanted him to be only in hopes that I would take the job he was RECRUITING me for. I specifically said, "I don't want anything you have to offer me," to let the devil know that I was onto his schemes and I didn't want his stuff or anything he was offering me.

John 10:10 says that the enemy comes to steal, kill, and destroy; he has no other plan but to do these things to our purpose and our future. The enemy plans to derail us from the purposes of God. Do you think that God would present you with a relationship that came to deceive you?

We did not meet on a dating app, he wasn't able to read my profile on social media, so how on earth was he able to deceive me? The truth is this: the devil studies us. He has no idea what our future holds, he is not omniscient like God, but he watches human patterns and he listens to what we say.

How can I be sure?

"Be alert and of sober mind. **Your enemy the devil prowls around like a roaring lion looking for someone to devour.**" (1 Peter 5:8)

Let's for a moment think about a lion's hunting strategy. It is said that most successful lion attacks happen at night - night can be a symbol of dark moments in your life.

A lion waits patiently for its prey to be alone, making them susceptible to an attack. This is why God encourages us in this verse to be alert and on guard for opportunities when the enemy uses people to attack us.

Not enough to convince you? Let's look at (Revelation 12:10 NIV). *"Then I heard a loud voice in heaven say: 'Now have come the salvation and the power and the kingdom of our God, and the authority of his Messiah. For the accuser of our brothers and sisters, who accuses them before our God day and night, has been hurled down."*

This verse from Revelation points to two things about our adversary: he is an accuser, and he doesn't sleep. An accuser's role is to bring up charges against the defendant. For someone to bring up charges against you, they must know your history, this clues us to the fact that Satan watches us. The key to this story is that this man did not know me but Satan did. Satan used a willing vessel to carry out a plan of attack on my self-esteem, future marriage, and heart.

The second thing this scripture points to is that Satan doesn't sleep; he is relentless. It's the same tactic the devil used to try and tempt Jesus in the wilderness after he had fasted for 40 days and 40 nights. When someone fasts, the one thing we can assume about them is that they are most likely weak and hungry, but definitely vulnerable.

Satan knew this would be the *perfect* time to test Jesus, so he dared him to turn some stones into bread. Jesus answered, "It is written: *'Man shall not live on bread alone, but on every word that comes from the mouth of God.'[b]"* Then the devil took him to the holy city and had him stand on the highest point of the temple. *"If you are the Son of God,"* he said, *"throw yourself down. For it is written: '"He will command his angels concerning you, and they will lift you up in their hands, so that you will not strike your foot against a stone."* Jesus answered him, *"It is also written: 'Do not put the Lord your God to the test."* Again, the devil took him to a very high mountain and showed him all the kingdoms of the world and their splendor. ***"All this I will give you,"*** he said, *"if you will bow down and worship me."*

Along with tempting Jesus to turn stones into bread, he offered Jesus something else - the seven wonders of the world. This proves that the enemy can *bless* us too - but his blessings come with stipulations because he is a natural deceiver.

Knowing the truth of this scripture, I was able to stand on Jesus's words and tell Satan I did not want anything he was offering me. Also, I do not want any counterfeit man he sends my way. Although waiting is not easy, I'd rather wait on God's best than the enemy's substitute.

Ladies, the enemy will send men into your life that look, sound, act, and even smell like husband material but aren't. This is why it is important to pray for discernment.

The enemy's imitation can never compare to God's original. Wait on God, continue to cast down these imaginations and "what-ifs" and make them come under God's subjection. Pray for God to close any open doors and remove any soul ties in your life.

"Casting down imaginations, and every high thing that exalteth itself against the knowledge of God and bringing into captivity every thought to the obedience of Christ." (2 Corinthians 10:5 KJV)

Be mindful of what your mind creates when you're dating. We create idols in our minds, and we worship them without realizing it. Allow God to speak to you about said gentleman before you allow him to take residence in your heart. Ask God if he's the one, then wait patiently for the answer and God will speak.

I speak to many single women about dating and relationships. One thing that is consistent among all the women that I speak to, who desire relationships, is that they all ignored the red flags. We ignore the signs that say he is emotionally unavailable, not ready for a commitment, and not connected to God.

In all of the situationships I've allowed myself to enter into, I can't say that I was ever bamboozled, I was just "thirsty."

REFLECTION

Some men will study you, listen to what you say, and attempt to mold themselves into what they think you desire. In some cases, it is obvious, in others not so much. In this social media world, it is easy for a man to look at your page, read your captions + your bio, study the places you've been to, see your friends, and listen to the things you talk about in your Insta stories, and then formulate what they think you want in their minds.

As women of God, we need to equip ourselves with discernment. Being able to determine whether a relationship is from God or just a distraction sent from the enemy is vital. Once your discernment signals that something isn't right, listen,

Sis. Don't be like the woman at the well, thirsty for things apart from God. You are not desperate.

LET'S PRAY

Heavenly Father, thank you for the gift of discernment and the Holy Scriptures who reveals your will to me. I do not have to navigate singleness blindly. Thank you for caring for me so much that you prompt me when things aren't lining up.

You are very intentional when it comes to me and I thank you for that. Help me to not only see the signs but to oblige to what you have revealed.

Remove all self-worthlessness and doubt that would encourage me to settle. You have great things in store for me. I decree and declare that I will be a recipient of your very best.

11.

Dating Yourself

A few years ago, a guy I was dating asked me what my interests and hobbies were. I was 20-something years old, and I had none to name. I was embarrassed that I didn't know what my interests were (aside from shopping). It was at that moment that I committed to starting to date myself. Don't be that woman who finds her purpose solely in a relationship. Don't allow your life to be completely wrapped up in your future spouse's.

When I left a long-term relationship, I had to discover who Sade was outside of being with another individual. My identity had been so wrapped up in my relationship that I didn't know what things I liked to do by myself. Marriage is an intimate lifelong relationship with another human, and it makes me wonder why we don't choose to spend the years available to us before marriage developing an intimate lifelong relationship with ourselves and with God.

But it is never too late to start, so here's some advice for my fellow single sisters: before you get into a relationship with another individual, have a life of your own. Discover yourself! Find out what things you're good at! Be goal-oriented! Driven! Motivated! You attract a good man to yourself when you have identified your worth, know yourself, and are walking in your purpose. All these things prepare you to be a true helpmate. Here are a few questions that might help you discover what you enjoy doing by yourself:

What do you like to do?

What hobbies do you have?

What interests you?

What drives you?

What activities fulfill you, and bring you happiness?

Dating Yourself Practically

When I first became single, I couldn't imagine going anywhere alone. The sheer thought of eating alone at a restaurant with everyone "watching," made me cringe. Now, I love my alone time. While I do occasionally have bouts of loneliness,

I also like my own company. And after the embarrassment of not being able to identify my hobbies, I decided that year to find out what my interests were and to start doing more of the things I liked. I discovered that:

- I love traveling alone. I love to plan trips and have everything completely mapped out before I go. I love to get up and do the things I want to do without having to wait for or depend on someone.
- I love shopping alone. Okay, this may be on every woman's list but I discovered that I find what I need when I am alone. I get super anxious when I'm shopping with other people. I'm the kind of shopper who goes through every single item on the rack to find the best deal (it's kind of my thing).
- I like to write. I never saw myself as a writer, but I really do enjoy writing. I've always been interested in research since my undergraduate school days. However, I didn't think it would translate into blogging, journaling, and writing this book. Getting thoughts down on paper has been very therapeutic for me over the past few years. I write letters to God and my future husband.
- I love to eat and cook. Cooking is my love language, it's a form of self-expression for me. I feel most creative when I am in the kitchen cooking up a new meal.

Okay, enough about me; I think you get the point! Simply stated, you mustn't allow your single years to pass you by without discovering who YOU are and what gets you going. This is a very important time in your life; don't let it simply pass you by.

Dating Yourself Spiritually

Learning how to date myself by doing the things I enjoy has been amazing, however learning about your spiritual self will sustain you. When I think about dating oneself, from a spiritual perspective, I think of uncovering an identity, discovering who you are at your core.

Your identity as a Christian starts with your understanding of who you are to God and in His kingdom. When we confess our salvation and receive Jesus Christ as our Lord and Savior, we become adopted into the Kingdom of God. We become a member of the family of other Christians. As with any family and kingdom, there are benefits, ordinances, and expectations. You must realize who you are to God. There are many biblical promises in scriptures that help to put context to this. John 1:12 ESV says:

> But to all who did receive him, who believed in his name, he gave the right to

become children of God. You are a child of God, as a child of God; you have God as your Father.

Galatians 4:3-7. [added for emphasis]:

"So also, when we were underage, we were in slavery under the **elemental spiritual forces of the world**. But when the set time had fully come, God sent his Son, born of a woman, born under the law, to redeem those under the law, **that we might receive adoption to sonship**. Because you are his sons [daughters], God sent the Spirit of his Son into our hearts, the Spirit who calls out, "Abba, Father." So you are no longer a slave, but God's child; and since you are his child, God has made you also an heir.

This is an excerpt from Paul's letter to the Church at Galatia. Here, he emphasizes that before we knew and accepted Christ, we were subject to the world's shifts, elements, changes, and powers but we are now heirs to God because we have accepted Christ. An heir is someone who is entitled to property after a person's passing. What does this mean for us? This illustrates that we are not illegitimate nor are we orphaned, we are God's children, and He has promises that are our right to receive. When we look at who we are in Christ, it will cause us to operate in this world very differently. When we know that we are fearlessly and wondrously made in God's image, He made no mistake in creating us, we can operate from a bolder stance. The way that I navigate relationships with men changed when I started to accept my position as an heir.

When I became set free from abandonment and rejection and recognized how much God loved me, I operated differently. I can attest that uncovering our identity is no easy feat; it takes time and patience. It involves healing from abandonment and recognizing who you are in Christ. It means giving yourself grace for the mistakes you made when you weren't operating in your full identity, accepting your position as heir to the King of Kings, and walking in your royalty. Your identity is not defined by how people see or treat you; your identity is defined by what the Word of God says about you. In God's words are the truths about who you are and what God's promises are to you.

I will never forget the moment my assignment in the kingdom of God was confirmed. I had just recently accepted Jesus Christ as my Lord and Savior and I was a member of the first church that I attended.

One day, a minister visited from out of state; this was my first time seeing a woman operate in the position of leadership in the church. After delivering a powerful message to the congregation, she offered to pray for anyone who desired it. As I saw people start to slowly stand up and walk up to the front of the church, one by one and then in groups, I sat in the pew, hands between my legs contemplating.

I was too afraid to walk to the front of this 300-member church. But before I knew it, I was at the altar. I watched as she spoke in a foreign language, that I later determined to be tongues, and laid hands on the members as she prayed for them. I stood at the back of the line adjacent to the stage waiting to get called. I waited for what seemed like an hour, certain they didn't see me standing there. In my head I kept hearing, "go sit down, go sit down," but my feet wouldn't move. I was the last one to be prayed for and now my fears had come true because I was the last one standing there, everyone else had gone back to their seats, and all eyes were on me.

I don't remember her exact prayer, but these eight words will never leave my memory, "You will be the mouthpiece to the nations." She laid her hands on me as she spoke, and before I knew it, I was on the floor. I had fallen flat. As I lay there on the floor, completely confused by what had just happened, I was so embarrassed. *How do I walk back to my seat after falling flat on the ground?* I asked myself. *Maybe I should just lay here until the service is over,"* I thought.

Someone eventually came to help me stand up, but I share this story with you because I believe that this is when the shame of my calling was born.

From that point forward, I remembered her words, but I just didn't know how to apply them to my life. What does it mean to be the voice of the nation and how do I get there? I was just *"coming to the faith,"* the only thing I knew at that point was the *"Lord's Prayer."* How in the world would I be a voice to the nations? I kept this in the back of my mind as I navigated through my church experience.

As I got plugged into the church community, I noticed that I had a high sense of discernment. I could determine the motives of others very quickly and easily. I began to even foretell future events to people and they'd come true. My dreams were vivid, and they were foretelling of things to come. I would have a strong knowledge of what to do and I had a sharp keenness for the voice of God. I thought this was every believer's experience, but as I journeyed on, I realized that it was not. God was slowly revealing to me that I was called to be a Prophet.

Due to my experience with other "prophets" in the body of Christ, I ran very far away from my calling. You may be thinking, what does this have to do with dating, marriage, and relationships? A lot! For ten years, I hid my gifts from crowds. I would only prophesy to close friends and family members for the most part. One day, after an intense season of spiritual warfare and persecution, I finally accepted my call. I cried intensely because this was not something I wanted. I read the story of the prophets in the Old Testament, and I began to understand their mandates and the effects of their calling. I recognized that they were hated and persecuted because of their role in the world. The purpose of accepting my calling is that I was finally rid of the shame and able to step into my full identity. My perspective of life changed. I began to think differently about my life goals, and I had to make necessary adjustments in my life.

Who we are is very important to God. Do not neglect to take the time in your singleness to discover this. We are to know who we are in order to operate in integrity in the relationships and friendships we are in. If we do not know who we are, the world will do a great job at telling us. Sis, you are more than simply a wife; God has a purpose for you.

> For just as each of us has one body with
> many members, and these members do
> not all have the same function, so in
> Christ we, though many, form one body,
> and each member belongs to all the

others. We have different gifts, according to the grace given to each of us. If your gift is prophesying, then prophesy in accordance with your[a] faith; if it is serving, then serve; if it is teaching, then teach; if it is to encourage, then give encouragement; if it is giving, then give generously; if it is to lead, do it diligently; if it is to show mercy, do it cheerfully. (Romans 12: 4-7 NIV)

When you don't take time to discover who you are, you become susceptible to allowing the world and relationships to define you!

REFLECTION

You matter to God. You have a purpose and an identity that is wrapped up in your Creator. He knows you intricately, everything about you. You are not here by happenstance. You are not a mistake. Sis, with the knowledge of this, I want to encourage you to lean into who God has called you to be.

Don't allow this single season (yes, it is only a season), to just pass you by. Take this grace period and get intentional about discovering who you are, what you are called to do, and what brings you joy.

Date yourself. Be available for the things you enjoy doing. Today fades, and tomorrow is upon us, so embrace this season. You will never be here again.

LET'S PRAY

Blessed God, I thank you that I am fearfully and wondrously made in your image. You know me so well that the very hairs on my head are numbered. You know me intricately. I am not a mistake. I am here for a reason.

Help me to lean into you and discover what that is. Give me the wisdom to uncover my purpose on earth and to walk boldly in that. Thank you for being patient with me. I give you permission to step in and guide me down the path that you have for me. I trust you with my life. My single season is not in vain. it will make sense in time and help me to embrace this truth in Jesus' name. Amen.

12.

Dear Single Woman, You are not alone

When I lost my paternal aunt in 2020, it came as the biggest shock of my life. So many were perishing due to the COVID-19 virus, but I never expected that I would lose someone too. My heart was broken because I expected God to heal my aunt and He didn't. I felt let down, heartbroken, and alone.

During that time, so many people reached out to offer me condolences saying, "You are not alone." It was as if God sent out a memo to let everyone know to call me and say those words. I didn't realize how much I needed to hear them, because that is exactly how I felt; alone. Even with the crowds of people around me and my 20k+ following on Instagram, I still felt very alone.

That loneliness drew me back into very disappointing feelings about my singleness. It was as if the pain and disappointment about my aunt's passing stirred up with the pain and disappointment of being single. Just like grief is said to come in waves, so does loneliness in singleness. It wasn't that I had not addressed these feelings before and come to a feeling of peace with God about it, it was simply the reality of the journey.

Josh Sherman and Steven Musso wrote a song called Psalm 23 (I Am Not Alone), derived from the well-known scripture, Psalm 23 "The Lord is My Shepherd." This song became the soundtrack of that season for me.

You have probably recited Psalm 23 countless times, but have you taken the time to truly understand what God's position as a Shepherd truly looks like?

Biblically, a shepherd's role was not only to tend to the needs of his sheep. He was to protect, guide, and feed his flock. Sheep are known to be unintelligent animals vulnerable and susceptible to death if not led by a shepherd. If a sheep leaves the flock and wanders, they are at risk of being slaughtered by wolves.

A good Shepherd understands this and does everything in their power to properly protect his sheep. The rod and staff that are mentioned in Psalm 23 are the instruments that the shepherd uses to navigate his flock forward and pull wandering sheep away from danger.

So when we think about God as the Good Shepherd, a very clear picture of his love, care, protection, and concern for us should be apparent. In this, we have the reassurance that God's role is to help us in our most vulnerable moments in our singleness. He will never leave us alone.

> Yea, though I walk through the valley of the shadow of death, I will fear no evil; for Thou art with me; Thy rod and Thy staff, they comfort me. (Psalm 23:4 KJV)

Lean into Your Community.

Grief hit me hard when I lost my aunt. This forced me to rely on others for comfort. There were days when I felt so overwhelmed with emotion that I would just call a friend to cry, and sometimes just lay on the phone in silence. I needed help, I needed community. It was during this season that I realized that I couldn't journey through life's challenges alone and I didn't have to. You don't have to either.

Other women are experiencing the same emotions surrounding their singleness that you are. They feel alone, overlooked, and hopeless about the prospects of finding a spouse. Find your community and lean on them.

Singleness is a journey that can feel like you're walking in a valley of death. This valley of death can be symbolic of a season. It can feel like your promises for marriage have died. If you are currently in a single season, then I'm certain you understand this feeling.

You may be at peace for a few months, content with the portion God has given you, glued tight to God's word, confident that God will come through for you. You may have even told a few friends, like I have, that this is the year God will bring you your spouse.

And you may have truly believed it too, until the year passes and, still, nothing. And then you enter into this season where there are no amount of scriptures, prophetic words, or encouragement that help. You may feel confident that God has lied to you, that you've heard him incorrectly. You may feel like it will never happen for you, that you were crazy to think it would.

I know how all of those seasons feel because I have been there. I have been super confident that God would bring me a spouse, and then a few months later feel like it would never happen. It can also become very discouraging to feel this way, I understand. There is nothing wrong with craving companionship. There is nothing wrong with feeling all the feelings you feel, Sis.

Can I offer you those same words that have helped me navigate these rough waters of grief and singleness? The same words that Sherman and Musso emphasized in their song:

You are not alone!

I am you.

I get it, Sis. I understand what you are going through. I pray that you'll feel encouraged and know that you are not alone. I understand the pressure that comes from waiting. I understand how delay can feel like denial. When you are delayed, it often feels like God has forgotten you. I understand that desires can sometimes overtake you. You can't stop thinking about it and you can't stop thinking about how you want to stop thinking about it.

Don't let anyone shame you into feeling that desiring marriage and a family is wrong. Don't let anyone tell you: "Don't think about it and it'll come." Be real about your emotions, don't bury them. I can be certain of this: God will never give you a desire He cannot fulfill. In Psalm 37:4, David expresses: "Take delight in the LORD, and he will give you the desires of your heart."

This is a two-fold promise, it means that God will place desires in your heart that were not once there, and He will manifest those desires. "How can I be certain that God gave me those desires?" you may ask. God will never place a desire in your heart that goes against His word. He will never give you the desire to sin or get in a relationship that's already sinful (God will not tell you to date a married man). God will give you desires that line up with His truth, and desires that will bring honor to His name.

Another scripture to gain a better understanding of our desires concerning God's will is found in John 14.

> Whatever you ask in My name, **that will I do**, so that the Father may be glorified in the Son. If you ask Me anything in My name, **I will do it**. If you love Me, you will keep My commandments. (John 14:13-15 ESV)

God promises to give us whatever we ask for, but it must be asked for in His name. What does this mean? This means that God will grant us whatever is according to His will. He places the desire of His will in our hearts. The only way to be certain that our desires are from God is by checking to see that they agree with His word, then wait on the thing you are praying for to manifest. If what you are asking for is from God, how can He not answer? It can be complicated to discern God's will from ours, this is why Jesus instructs us in Matthew to ask for God's will to be done when we pray. Asking for God's will to be done in your life is the best way to leave your desires in God's hands.

God is not a god of broken promises. So as we wait for our spouse, the best thing we can do is put our faith in God. I pray that while you wait, God will bring every one of your desires to life. I pray that God will give you the ability to discern His will from your desires and the grace to wait on His very best. I pray that you will close out this chapter of the book feeling seen and understood. You are not alone.

REFLECTION

I can still feel the weight lifting from my shoulders as I heard the psalmist sing the words: "You are not alone." These four words were echoed through the voices of so many during my season of grief. I still take comfort in the awareness that I do not have to brave life's challenges alone, especially the valleys of singleness. God is our Great Shepherd who takes pleasure in attending to our needs.

LET'S PRAY

Heavenly Father, to the woman reading this, I pray that you remind her that you are the Good Shepherd who carefully tends to the needs of His sheep. Comfort her in this dark season of her singleness where she feels most alone. Remind her that she is not forgotten by you. Let the words of this chapter wash over her and bring her comfort. Thank you for protecting her from relationships that mean her no good.

Bring peace to her mind and aching heart. Thank you for chasing her down, even now, to show her your great compassion and care for her. She is the one that you left the pack to tend to.

Thank you for your attentive care of her needs. You will not allow her to be led astray; you have rescued her and reminded her of your nature. You are a God who comforts her in her most vulnerable moments. Your love and compassion for her never fail. While she continues to wait, please reassure her that what she's waiting for is possible. Help her to endure this season by restoring her hope.

In Jesus' name. Amen.

13.

Sex is Not a Curse Word

I think we all have memories from our childhood of our first introduction to sex. I would hope that your experience was not as traumatic as mine because mine started at the early age of 8

I remember my fourth-grade teacher interrupting her lesson to tell me that my father was at the school to see me. As I walked into the elementary school stairway, I saw my cousin looking extremely nervous and my father pacing from side to side.

"Did Mr. Brown touch you?" he asked, in a panic, followed by, "because if he did, I am going to get a gun and kill him." Knowing my father's rage and desire to protect me, I knew he wasn't kidding. I began to cry and stutter over my words as I exclaimed, "No, what are you talking about?"

He proceeded to tell me that a close friend's father was being accused of inappropriately touching young girls in the neighborhood. "You better not be lying to me," he exclaimed. I truthfully told him I wasn't, and he and my cousin dashed down the stairs.

I grew up in a home where sexual misconduct was experienced but not expressed. It was a "taboo" topic, so we didn't talk about it. Based on conversations with my friends, I've concluded that this is often the case in many Black homes, but these secret experiences go on to haunt the victims years after. This was my story too.

From the age of 8 until my early teens, I was molested by the same cousin who nervously stood by as my father questioned me in that elementary school staircase. At this time, the fear of sharing my secret intensified because my father threatened to kill Mr. Brown. I didn't know how to verbalize what had happened to me but based on this staircase conversation, I became aware that something was seriously wrong with how I was being touched.

One day, my dad took me on our usual trip to the Upper East Side, NYC, to watch a movie and enjoy hotdogs at Papaya's restaurant. Although sexual misconduct wasn't discussed in the home, my father always provided a safe space for us to have truthful and honest conversations about everything else. He was an open book. Growing up in the 80s during the crack and AIDS epidemic, he had lots of stories to share with me, so we spent most of our time together having deep and intellectual conversations. This is the one thing I miss a lot about my dad since his passing in 2018.

We were standing in the brightly lit Papaya's restaurant when I blurted out to my dad that my cousin had been inappropriately touching me. Much like a lot of my earlier experiences, I don't recall what he said, but I do remember him listening very intently as I shared my experience. Our next conversation about the molestation was my dad asking me if I wanted to speak to a counselor about what had transpired. I agreed to get counseling.

My dad eventually confronted my family about the molestation. Similar to experiences I've heard from other women, it went undiscussed from that point forward. We never brought it up again. We never discussed it in my home; it was as if it never happened. When conversations about sex are not had in the home, it leaves children having to figure it out on their own.

This *figuring-it-out- is*, in most cases, shaped by the media and other not-so-positive influences. I wish this weren't the case for me, especially when I realized that I'd developed an addiction to pornography and masturbation.

I don't remember my first experience with watching porn, but I do remember how much it controlled my thoughts. My days were consumed with thoughts of running home so that I could fill my evenings with watching pornography. I was a slave to it. I recall being so consumed by the thoughts that I could barely focus on my classwork.

Before my father sought out counseling for me, I didn't know how to process my feelings. In counseling, I hid the deep and dark emotions tied to the molestation. I lived in shame. I was ashamed of what happened to me and carried the shame of my porn addiction and masturbation. How could I tell my parents this secret I was carrying?

I never did.

In fact, we did discuss sex or address the molestation outside the comforts of the therapist's office. When I told my mother that I had sex for the first time, she cried. Even then, the sex conversation never found its way into my home. I had to find out about sex on my own.

This obsession with pornography and perversion carried well into my adult years. My lust for pornography transformed into my obsession with sex with different men. I often found myself lusting after men. I wasn't too much interested in relationships, I just yearned for the feeling that came from sex.

I wish I had someone to share these thoughts with, but I didn't, the influence of my friends only pushed me deeper into sexual sin.

One-night stands were my thing. Pornography had painted such graphic images of sex in my mind that whenever I encountered a man my mind went there first. It was a cycle that while enjoyable at the time, was taking me so far out of God's will for me. I look back and thank God for preserving me through those years and not allowing me to experience something I would live to regret.

I think it's important that believers start being more transparent and honest about their lives before finding God. Or even about sharing some of the pitfalls they encountered while saved. Because we have so many preachers speaking at people and fleeing from vulnerability, I believe many women live in shame because of their past, or current struggles with sexual sin. I understand where many of you may be right now.

Even as you read this, you may be fighting to break a cycle of sexual sin that has you in bondage. It is not freeing. People can call it what they want to, but sin is anything that God despises, and it keeps us separate from him and keeps us bound. I was in bondage to pornography, masturbation, and pre-marital sex. Because molestation opened the door to these things, the enemy was able to keep me bound for years. It wasn't until God broke me free that I even realized that those things were not even true desires of mine. By partnering with God, I was able to discover what I truly desired, a marriage and a family with my husband.

Honestly, I believe that God transformed my mind and gave me new desires. Desires that are fulfilling and satisfying.

Because sex is also not a popular topic of discussion within Church culture, we often come up with our own ideas of what sex is. As believers, if these ideas are not aligned with any biblical text, it can be very dangerous. Where do your ideas about what sex is come from? I hope that a clear biblical perspective on sex will relieve you of the shame you may have attached to it. Additionally, scientific knowledge on the implications of sex can help eradicate some of the lies you've come to believe. Let's dive in!

The Biblical Purpose of Sex

To understand sex, it is important to go to the creator of sex and what He has to say about it in the Bible. Surprisingly, God did not and does not shy away from the topic of sex. The first mention of sex in the Bible is ironically found in Genesis, the first book of the bible. In Genesis 1:28, God gave us the first fundamental purpose of sex and sex in marriage:

> *And God blessed them, and God said unto them, Be fruitful, and multiply, and replenish the earth, and subdue it: and*

have dominion over the fish of the sea, and
over the fowl of the air, and over every
living thing that moves upon the earth.

God granted the first man and woman permission to procreate and, in order to procreate, at least in Biblical days, sex was part of the equation. Through sex, Adam and Eve would multiply and replenish the earth. God created sex to multiply the earth and to subdue and have dominion over the earth. Sex was never created to subdue us. God gave us authority – permission to rule with our spouses. Sex was given as both a gift and a promise from God. Not only does sex have a purpose, but sex is also good because everything God created is good. We can be certain of that because a beautiful reassurance is tucked in a verse in Genesis.

Then God saw EVERYTHING that He had made, and indeed it was very good. (Genesis 1:31a NASB)

If everything that God created was very good, then God's method for multiplying and populating the world is also good. When speaking about sex, I cannot neglect to discuss intimacy. If you are single and abstaining from sex like myself then I'm sure that intimacy is something you are missing right now.

When in conversation with my girlfriends, a lot of what I hear isn't: "I miss having sex" but rather "I miss having a man around." What they are missing is the intimacy of a relationship.

A year into the pandemic I remember telling a friend of mine that I was craving testosterone, I wanted to be around masculine energy. The friend dates plus hour-long conversations with my girlfriends had grown old and tired. I needed some masculine energy. It wasn't that I wanted sex entirely, that was about 60%, but what I craved was intimacy: physical and emotional closeness. I missed handholding, forehead kisses, late-night cuddles, the feeling of being desired and loved, vulnerability, and expressions of trust in conversation. I missed it all. I was willing to accept cat-calling if that meant feeling desired for a second, I was desperate.

A biblical perspective of intimacy is expressed in Genesis 2: *"Therefore shall a man leave his father and his mother, and shall cleave unto his wife: and they shall be one flesh."* (Genesis 2:24 KJV)

Gill's exposition of the Bible paints a beautiful description of what cleaving looks like: "...and shall cleave unto his wife; with a cordial affection, taking care of her, nourishing and cherishing her, providing all things comfortable for her, continuing to live with her, and not depart from her as long as they live: the phrase is expressive of the near union by marriage between man and wife; they are, as it were, glued together, and make but one..."

How much more intimate can marriage be if God's instruction is for our future husbands to cleave to us and become one flesh. That sounds pretty close to me, Sis. I look at this verse as a promise God has made to us, and as something that we can look forward to in marriage. I am ready to cleave! How about you?

Misconceptions About Sex

When we read further into the book of Genesis, we are introduced to Satan. His role is to both deceive us and pervert everything God created. Sex was not off the table in his deception and perversion agenda. His very first encounter with humans was to deceive and pervert God's intention for humankind. This deception is illustrated in the story of Adam and Eve in the book of Genesis.

The enemy came to Eve and lured her into eating from the tree God had forbidden them to eat from. Eve and Adam were deceived and tempted by Satan to disobey God. This subsequently brought sin (separation) from God into the world. Satan did not stop in Genesis. His plot to deceive humanity and distort everything God created for good into bad was a secondary running theme in the Bible.

In our contemporary world, his perversion of sex is particularly perpetuated through media. We have developed a misconstrued idea of love and sex, and we have strayed away from its original intent. God created sex to be very good and the purpose of it was for us to come together with our spouses, to procreate, develop intimacy, for pleasure, and to rule and subdue the earth.

There is a purpose to sex, but if churches are not having conversations about sex and our parents are tiptoeing around talks of the "birds and the bees," where are we getting our knowledge from? Our friends? The media? Trauma? Through conversations I have had with women about sex, I learned that most have developed a lot of misconceptions about it. Myself included! Here are some of them.

Sex means Commitment

Women crave stability, commitment, and consistency, and these are certainly in the top ten of my list. My experiences and constant disappointments with men have shown me how deeply I value consistency and commitment. When we are having sex outside the confines of marriage, we can confuse a man who is committed to having sex with a man who is committed to us. A man who is committed to having sex with you does not mean he is committed to you.

I have found that when we jump straight into sex, we miss a lot of red flags. Having sex with a man does not increase his desire to marry you. Commitment is truly a heart's desire. Sex does not equal love. We ought to not simply accept or settle for a man who is committed to having sex with us when we desire commitment in marriage.

I was sexually involved with my ex for seven years. I think the sex is what kept us together, but it didn't make him more committed to me. I desired marriage and he desired sex, so when sex was off the table, his commitment to me was too. This was a huge pill for me to swallow, but I am grateful that I learned this in my singleness and not in a marriage. It takes more than just sex to keep relationships together, I am sure this is something with which you can agree.

Sex will create intimacy which will help you keep a man

While a man may stay and be emotionally intimate if you are engaging in premarital sex, we cannot assume that sex will make him stay. If you desire a kingdom marriage where Jesus is at the center, then it is important to do it Jesus's way. It is better to create intimacy with the one God has for you. Many women are in relationships where they feel the burden of having to "keep a man" by having to give up a piece of themselves to do so. This is not God's will for us. We deserve better.

Sex is for domination

I don't remember my first introduction to pornography, but it was before my young mind could comprehend what sex was. The overdramatization of sex in pornography distorted my perception of sex. Pornography created unattainable images of sex. There are no boundaries with sex in pornography, anything goes, and I am not surprised that some women perceive sex as a tool for domination. We can agree that sex is a good gift from God to unify us with our husbands.

Sex is just a fun pastime that will make you feel better

When I began to explore the intricacies of sex and its effects on the body and the brain, I realized that the phrase "It's just sex" diminishes the power that sex truly has. Desiring marriage but constantly settling for sex is not fun. Dealing with the scars that are left after every premarital sexual encounter is not fun. The emptiness that we feel after we've given ourselves to another man, with no promise of marriage, is not fun.

Staying connected to a man and having our souls knit together is not fun.

Sex is bad

I was surprised to learn how prevalent this thought is amongst fellow believers. Listen, we are not an afterthought to God and neither was his creation of sex. The opposite of this statement is the truth, sex is good. How can I be certain? In Genesis 1:31 New Living Translation (NLT), *"Then God looked over all he had made, and he saw that it was very good! And evening passed and morning came, marking the sixth day."* God looked over all he had made and saw that it was good, sex is included in this. Everything that comes from God is good. A few scriptures that point to this are:

He is the Rock, His work is perfect; all His ways are just. (Deuteronomy 32:4)

Therefore listen to me, you men of understanding. Far be it from God to do wrong, and for the Almighty to act unjustly. (Job 34:10 NASB)

They will declare, "The LORD is just! He
is my rock! There is no evil in him!"
(Psalm 92:15 NLT)

Sex is love

If we turn on any romantic comedy, the chances are
that a love connection is triggered at the onset by sex.
After that first night of passion, the actors on screen are
deeply in love. What we don't often realize are the
seeds that are planted through watching these stories
over and over. This is where our desires are bred.

My ex-boyfriend could not fathom the thought
of going without sex until marriage. To be honest, I
couldn't myself. When I decided to become abstinent, I
don't think I gave the *whole* giving up sex thing a
thought.

But when I look back at the toxicity of our
relationship and think about the conversations we had
about sex, I am reminded of how my ex often equated
sex with love. "If you love me, you would have sex with
me," was a common and manipulative phrase he would
often use to pressure me into having sex with him. His
idea of sex was quite delusional and problematic.
Having been exposed to sex at a young age, I can
understand why these misconceptions are so

prevalent. My view of sex was also perverted, with trauma woven into my story based on my own experience.

However, this is a common misconception about love. The truth is that sex does not equate to love. If God is love, and we are not having sex with God then what does that say? I know this may be foreign and uncomfortable, but this *is* the reality.

I believe choosing pre-marital sex helps us form a bond with someone while unfortunately disregarding the red flags. Of course, before scientists discovered oxytocin and researchers developed theories on its bonding capabilities (functions), God through scriptures expressed a clear biblical truth about soul ties, we cannot ignore both the biblical and the scientific implications.

I will try to explain as best as I can in the next few pages what all of this means.

What in the World is a Soul Tie?

Have you been involved with someone, who wasn't good for you, but then you had a difficult time breaking it off with them? In the natural sense, you may have looked at the experience as a "bad break-up," in the spiritual sense, however, what you didn't realize was that sex knits your soul to another individual and creates a soul tie. Breaking up rips that knitting apart, making it hurt. When we are sexually involved with someone, we give them a piece of ourselves.

The first mention of soul ties in the Bible is in Genesis 2:24 with Adam and Eve. After God created all the world, He gave Adam the task of naming the animals, and then God declared that it is not good for man, Adam, to be alone. There was no suitable helpmate for Adam found in all of God's creation, hence God put Adam to sleep and created Eve from his rib. After this miracle, the word of God says: "That is why a man leaves his father and mother and is **united** to his wife, and they become **one flesh**." In the union between husband and wife, under God's covenant, they become ONE flesh; they're knit together by God.

The second reference to soul ties is In the book of Samuel. We learn of two men, Jonathan, and David, who were friends. *"And it came to pass, when he had made an end of speaking unto Saul, that the soul of Jonathan was knit with the soul of David, and Jonathan loved him as his own soul."(*1 Samuel 18:1 KJV.)

Their souls were knit together. In this case, the soul tie between Jonathan and David was based on a friendship.

Another mention of this knitting of souls together is in 1 Corinthians 6:16, *"Do you not know that he who unites himself with a prostitute is one with her in body? For it is said, "The two will become one flesh."* Sex knits inside and outside of marriage and unites people. For many, this may be a foreign topic, but chances are it's not a foreign experience. If you've engaged in pre-marital sex, you have probably experienced an ungodly soul tie that has kept you from seeing clearly, and, also, when a breakup occurs, it burns.

One clear scientific implication of sex is the chemical release of oxytocin during intercourse. Oxytocin is a hormone that is found in humans and other animals. Some of its functions are to stimulate birth contractions during labor, stimulate lactation during breastfeeding, and promote maternal bonding. For years, oxytocin has been infamously named the "love hormone" or the "cuddle hormone," because while it plays a key role in childbirth and post-childbirth mother and child bonding, it also plays an important role in human sexual interactions.

Oxytocin is a bonding hormone that is released during sex to allow partners to bond together. It is the agent that chemically unites you with another individual during intercourse. This is how intentional God is. He said it is not good for a man to be alone and created a helpmate for him. God encouraged man and his helpmate to procreate. Through the release of oxytocin, the man and his helpmate are chemically bound together to fulfill God's promise.

The bond that is created when having sex is not always evidence of love as defined in 1 Corinthians 13 but rather evidence of a chemical connection that bonds sexual partners together and keeps them connected. However, it can make it easy for us to confuse love with lust.

In her book, *The Chemistry of Connection: How the Oxytocin Response Can Help You Find Trust, Intimacy, and Love,* author Susan Kuchinskas writes: "... when the intoxicating neurochemicals of romance have ebbed, the oxytocin released during sex reinforces the bond and helps us weather the inevitable annoyances and hardships of living with someone and raising a family." The hormones released during sex are intended to help a husband and wife stay connected even when the flutters have simmered.

When we choose to have premarital sex with an individual, we can create a bond or tie that is not often easy to break.

Soul ties can cause you to lust after an individual you should no longer be with. Have you caught yourself saying: "For some reason, I cannot end the relationship?" "There is something that is keeping me with him," or "there is *just* something that won't let me leave?" That "something" is a soul tie.

Sis, it's not just that the sex with him was good, let's not minimize what God intended when he created sex. Sex with our husbands was created to be an act to unite us.

If we are having sex with someone who isn't our husband this does not negate God's design of it, hard truth I know. I had to come to this understanding myself. Because I was never one who openly connected with my emotions, I figured I could have sex and "not catch feelings." This wasn't possible. Even years after some of my "friends with benefits" relationships ended; I was plagued by the memories of our encounters. This is not something I desire to take into my marriage. This is not something I want to hold on to in my singleness.

Imagine this for a moment. You are lying in bed with your husband and you are replaying the memories of your past sexual experience in your mind. Imagine still longing for or comparing your husband to your last sexual experience. This isn't fair to you or your future husband. This is something I want no part of. I've heard the story of married women who have experienced this, desiring men who weren't their husbands because of unsevered soul ties. This can lead to infidelity and a lack of intimacy.

Your soul may be connected to someone right now. Maybe you've had difficulty shaking off that past relationship. If you've lived long enough, you've probably made many choices that aren't the best, and those choices have consequences. Pre-marital sex is not a good choice and soul ties are one consequence of that choice.

> "Do you not know that your body is a
> temple of the Holy Spirit who lives in
> you, whom you have received from God?
> (John 14: 15-17)

According to 1 Corinthians 6:19, "You are not your own." Premarital sex leaves us feeling the shame of ties with people that we cannot break; I've been there before. Thank God for Jesus who delivers us and saves us and does not condemn us. I encourage you to start truly living for God and being wiser about the choices you make.

So now what?

REFLECTION

I want to help you renounce any soul ties. Biblically, These are the steps you can take if you want to renounce a soul tie.

1. Acknowledge - this is where you identify and accept that you have an ungodly soul tie with another individual.
2. Repent + Renounce
3. Forgive

This is by no means a comprehensive list of all the steps you can take to renounce a soul tie. They are however the key steps you can take in any acts you may have committed that were displeasing in the sight of God.

This is a common thread throughout the word of God. We are constantly in a state of repentance. This is for you, Sis. This is nothing to feel ashamed or embarrassed about, I want you to be free. I speak to too many women who suffer in silence about these soul ties. They are constantly plagued with dreams and memories of past relationships. They want to be free but don't know where to find that freedom.

It's in Christ.

He wants the same for you, Beloved. No longer will you be held captive to a relationship that didn't work.

No longer will you be in bondage to memories of past sexual experiences.

From this point forward, you are free. Walk boldly in the liberty of knowing that Christ has set you free. Partner with a friend who will hold you accountable + get plugged into a community that will help you live out this walk of freedom. Remember, you are not alone. You are not without hope + help. You have taken the first step and I believe that God will help you move forward.

LET'S PRAY

Dear God, thank you for giving me insight into what a soul tie is. Thank you for giving me your word to stand on as your truth. Thank you for giving me the wisdom and discernment to make better choices in my life. I desire to be pleasing in your sight so that I do not miss out on any of your blessings. Lord, I come before you at this moment renouncing any soul ties with any individuals I have had sex with outside of the covenant of marriage. I say their names out loud, one by one, and I decree that by the blood of Jesus that the tie is broken. No more chains holding me, no more shame, no more oppression, no more tormenting thoughts, and no more sleepless nights.

In the name of Jesus, it is broken, and by your power, I will never return. I am free. The word of God says that where the spirit of the Lord is, there is liberty! 2 Corinthian 3:17.

Thank you, Lord. Amen.

14.

Why I said No to Sex and Yes to God

It was 2013, and I had just made a huge career change. Life as I knew it had changed. A lot of things in my life were changing, for the best, but nothing could prepare me for this disruption. I was in a 7-year relationship with my college boyfriend, and there was no doubt in my mind that we were going to get married. After all, that is what all long-term relationships lead to, right?

Wrong!

I did not know what marriage entailed, nor did I understand God's view on marriage then. I knew nothing about communication or compromise, or my readiness for a lifetime commitment. However, even though we had a rocky and immature relationship - we were two kids taking a stab at lust - I believed he was "the one." Unbeknownst to me, I was dealing with the effects of underlying abandonment and rejection issues and was in no position to be anyone's wife.

Then one night, I was awakened out of my sleep by a dream, and that dream was the trigger that changed the trajectory of my life. In my dream, my grandmother was presenting me with two shirts to wear. Both were blue, but one had images of crosses all over it, and the other did not.

She asked me to choose a shirt. "I think I like the shirt with the crosses on it!" I said. She said, "You can either wear this plain blue shirt or this blue shirt with the crosses on it! With this shirt covered in crosses, you are blessed and covered. You are blessed going in and blessed going out. You will never have to worry about another situation in your life!" I cried tears of joy knowing I made the right decision!

When I woke up out of my dream, I had Deuteronomy 28 (NLT) in my heart! I had never read Deuteronomy, but God placed this exact scripture in my heart.

> "If you fully obey the Lord your God and carefully follow all his commands I give you today, the Lord your God will set you high above all the nations on earth. All these blessings will come on you and accompany you if you obey the Lord your God. You will be blessed in the city and blessed in the country. The fruit of your womb will be blessed, and the crops of your land and the young of your livestock—the calves of your herds and the lambs of your flocks. Your basket and your kneading trough will be blessed. You will be blessed when you come in

and blessed when you go out. The Lord will grant that the enemies who rise up against you will be defeated before you. They will come at you from one direction but flee from you in seven. The Lord will send a blessing on your barns and on everything you put your hand to. The Lord your God will bless you in the land he is giving you. The Lord will establish you as his holy people, as he promised you on oath, if you keep the commands of the Lord your God and walk in obedience to him. Then all the peoples on earth will see that you are called by the name of the Lord, and they will fear you. The Lord will grant you abundant prosperity—in the fruit of your womb, the young of your livestock, and the crops of your ground—in the land he swore to your ancestors to give you. The Lord will open the heavens, the storehouse of his bounty, to send rain on your land in season and to bless all the work of your hands. You will lend to many nations but will borrow from none. The Lord will make you the head, not the tail. If you pay attention to the commands of the Lord your God that I give you this day and carefully follow them, you will always be at the top, never at the bottom. Do not turn aside from any of the commands I give you today, to the right or to the left, following other gods and serving them." (Deuteronomy 28: 1-28.)

In verses 1-15, God speaks of the many blessings afforded to us if we choose to obey Him, and Deuteronomy 28 is filled with numerous "if, then" statements. I believe they are to encourage us to be obedient. If we are obedient to God and follow His commands, He must and will carry out every promise spoken in His word. God describes to us all how we will be blessed! He promises to grant us divine protection and manifest an abundance of blessings in our lives. The blessings that God promises us in Deuteronomy 28 will make us successful financially and spiritually. All these blessings are promised to us and the only requirement is that we obey the voice of God.

Pre-marital sex was the thing that was drawing a wedge between me and God. Listen, I know that sin is not a popular topic in today's world. Your favorite pastors and preachers are probably doing cartwheels around this topic on Sunday mornings. Regardless of how we dip and dodge it, the word of God is very clear on what is acceptable and what is not. Listen, I wanted to keep having sex just like the next twenty-something-year-old, but it was very clear what God was saying. My decision to obey God and give up sex until marriage was not something a prophet or parent told me to do, it came straight from God. The dream, the scripture, and the conviction all pointed to one thing, I had to say no to sex and yes to God.

If you've come this far in this book, you know that I am not a religious, legalistic person. I am in a relationship with God. When you have a relationship with someone, you desire to do things that please them and that's the difference here. The thing about sin is that it not only separates us from God, but it also separates us from the things of God. This is the illustration that God gave me with Deuteronomy 28. I didn't want to miss out on God's blessing because of sex. And looking back to the decision I made years ago, I can clearly see how I would've. I don't want you to.

Like a good father, God knows each one of us individually. "Indeed, the very hairs on your head are all numbered," he declares in Luke 12:7a. God created me to be ambitious, and he knows I naturally chase after every vision He gives me. When God shared His promises with me, He knew I would obey Him. I want to stress that God did not force my hand to obey Him, He gave me an option. The reason I need to stress this is because I want to emphasize the freedom of choice God gives us. We have free will to choose. God didn't create us to be robots, He created us with the capacity to reason and make our own choices. He knew that by giving me a glimpse of my future, I would set aside everything and follow Him. He also knew that the journey ahead would be exciting but challenging, and his promises kept me going.

Don't get me wrong, doubt crept into my mind. I wondered if I'd be able to maintain a vow of celibacy., but God gave me peace when He spoke these words to me, "*I have so much planned for you. You have a choice. You can give up premarital sex, follow me, and obtain all these blessings or you can stay in this relationship and miss out on EVERYTHING I HAVE FOR YOU.*"

Although the vision for my life flashed before me quite quickly, it was very detailed. I sensed it all and saw years of my life appear before my eyes in one moment. God revealed that I would eventually have a huge platform where my life would be on display. My life needed to align both with the word of God and the person I professed to be. I didn't need another vision or sign, I knew what God wanted me to do; I had to say "YES to God and NO, to sex."

Let's take a moment to pause and address how God speaks and how to hear from Him. I use the phrase "God spoke to me" quite often, and I recognize that this may be foreign to many. When it isn't foreign, many may not be able to discern the voice of God. If this is an area you are struggling in and want to be certain that God is speaking, I'd recommend trusting the small voice that you hear and start doing what you think you've heard.

When you first start to hear God's voice, it can be quite soft and quick but taking a small step of faith over and over again in the direction you hear Him call, sharpens your ability to discern between God's voice and yours. It will help you tune your ear to God.

For any believer, this is such an important fact that we must not overlook. The voice of God is not always a voice, sometimes, it is an inner knowing of something, often something you've never considered.

Have you ever had a random thought to do something? This can often be the prompting of the Holy Spirit or God's voice. We are all in different places in our faith journey, however, the inability to discern God's voice does not make you less of a Christian; the desire alone is pleasing to God. This ability to discern God's voice was a major help on my journey of singleness especially when it came to making tough decisions around sex, because

Sis, it was not easy.

You would think that after I chose to become abstinent, I wouldn't be met with opposition; well, at least that's what I thought. It was not the case.

On Valentine's Day in 2013, my boyfriend planned a dinner date at an expensive steak house in New York City. I knew that sex was going to be expected at the end of that date, and I had to prepare myself to have the tough conversation.

"I've decided to be abstinent," I blurted out over my medium-well steak, baked potatoes, and bread rolls.

"You what?" he asked. "How? What does this mean?"

The questions were unending, and the rest of the night was a complete blur. I knew the days ahead would be interesting, but I had made a vow with God, and I was unwilling to break it. Just as expected, the following days and weeks had me trying to explain my choice to "Say no to sex, and Yes, to God." My ex was not interested in being abstinent and was adamant about it. He said seemingly convincing things like: "God made us like this," "we are young," "we are in a relationship, we are supposed to have sex," "God will forgive us," and "He is a forgiving God." But I wasn't budging. I knew God's purpose for me was far greater than the satisfaction I received from sex, and I wasn't willing to remain in sin, reject God, and miss out on the future that God had for me.

"Am I supposed to just spend the rest of my life sinning because God will forgive me?" I asked. He had no answer.

What shall we say then? Shall we
continue in sin, that grace may abound?
(Romans 6:1 KJV)

This scripture would become the foundation scripture for the days ahead. I realized that God wants us to set aside fleshly desires and chase after Him, and He understands that our flesh (will) is weak. However, He encourages us to seek Him in moments of weakness.

> "My grace is sufficient for you, for my power is made perfect in weakness. Therefore I will boast all the more gladly about my weaknesses, so that Christ's power may rest on me." (2 Corinthians 12:9)

In this scripture, Paul recognizes that he was weak, and in His moments of weakness, he was able to see God's true strength. God steps in when we are at our point of weakness, and He shows us that we don't have to carry the weight of celibacy on our own.

It was only a matter of time before my ex and I began speaking different languages. When he realized I wasn't budging, he became distant. He wouldn't look at me, hug me, be affectionate with me or visit me. Phone calls got shorter, and text messages were very rare. Our relationship was fading, and someone had to make the final call – so, I ended it. I didn't choose to become abstinent as an ultimatum for him to marry me, however, I still found it heartbreaking that He never once mentioned marriage. That was when the thoughts of unworthiness started to creep in. *Had I been the one he wanted to marry? Was he even considering marriage? What was I doing all these years in this relationship? Was my body only a toy for his entertainment?* A part of me thought we could journey through this together, but I was wrong.

I often get asked this question: "What if I am abstinent and the man I am dating is not, what should I do?" Now, my opinion on this matter may differ from many others. They may not think that a difference in values regarding abstinence is that important. I don't agree. I don't believe it is beneficial to stay in a relationship with someone who does not have a biblical understanding and implications of premarital sex or who is willing to commit to God. Now, others may offer up the advice that the man can change; I can understand the perspective. In that case, I always recommend presenting your concerns to God, and He will guide you.

I have come to learn that men who do not desire to be abstinent are often not committed to their relationship with God. Imagine a man saying, I do not agree with what the bible says concerning marriage and sex. As a woman of God, what are you going to do with this information? When a man is uncommitted to living according to God's word, this is what He is saying. And if a man cannot be committed to God, how can he lead you? How? A man can be committed to a job but if that falls through then what happens? How can he lead if He doesn't have direction from God?

When I look at the life I lived after being saved, although I am not perfect, I had a desire to please God. The word of God says that you will know a tree by its fruit, so you will have to ask yourself: "What fruit is he bearing?" A man who is unwilling to give up sex until marriage is most likely battling a lust issue. I have met men on different points of the spectrum. You have the guy who is completely against abstaining from pre-marital sex who is also flaky in his relationship with God and then you have the one who is considering it but struggling. I would prefer the man I am dating to be clear and vocal about his thoughts on pre-marital sex. These are the tough conversations that we are often afraid to have that keep us in grey areas of confusion.

How a man prioritizes biblical principles says a lot about him. Another reason I cannot date a man who is not already abstaining from sex is that I don't have the self-control to do it alone. In some situations, the woman is the initiator of sex and has a lust issue she cannot manage; I have been this woman. Having been exposed to sex at a young age, I recognize that this is something that I struggle with. I was not given a chance to view sex as a sacred act, so when I was interested in a man in the past, it was sexually above everything else. Until God revealed to me, years into my abstinence, that He used abstinence as a way to protect me from myself.

The reality is this: If we are not dealing with our sin issue in our singleness, it will carry over into our marriage.

Overall, I desire a man to be as committed to his walk with God as I am. Is that asking for too much?

Maybe some of you are reading this thinking about the struggles you've had while deciding to abstain. Maybe you've even considered that abstinence isn't for you. I want to be clear that I am not here to condemn you. I am here to offer you a biblical perspective on sex and marriage. I want to offer you the truth from the word of God, this isn't "what Sade thinks." Abstinence is a heart choice; it is better made with your heart than your head. It is a covenant and vow between you and God. You cannot force someone to make a heart choice; they have to desire it for themselves. Your heart is where your motives and your desires lie. Matthew 6:21, "For where your treasure is, there your heart will be also."

REFLECTION

I will never forget the moment I decided to say yes to God and no to sex. I had no idea that that decision would be the catalyst to ending my 7-year relationship. As I reflect on that decision, years later, I can confidently say that I have no regrets. To be in a relationship with God is to be committed to God through our actions. The word of God is very clear when it comes to its perspective on premarital sex and marriage, there are no gray areas concerning this. Even though the Bible speaks of these matters, we can all probably agree that it doesn't always help our decision. The choice to obey God and hang up sex until marriage is not a head decision but rather a decision of the heart. Abstaining from sex on your own is hard. For this reason, when dating, it is essential to date someone whose values regarding the scriptures on sex and marriage align.

LET'S PRAY

God, thank you for stopping me in my tracks this day and sharing with me your thoughts concerning abstinence. It is a struggle. It is a struggle deciding to abstain and even a struggle to maintain my commitment to it, but I trust you. I trust your ability to help me navigate this journey of abstinence and singleness. I trust you to direct my steps and lead me to individuals that will hold me accountable. I do not want to miss out on the plans you have for me. Thank you for covering my shame today and giving me a chance to get this right. I pray that your commitment and compassion towards me will never fail. I pray that you equip me with the tools, plans, and resources that will help me maintain this vow to you. I trust that won't fail me in this area.

In Jesus' name. Amen.

15.

What's This Gonna Cost Me?

Jesus' ministry primarily began when He selected 12 men to join His team; twelve men he affectionately called disciples. Jesus was aware of his earthly mission to die for the sins of the world, and He was also aware that someone would need to carry out His mission after His death. So as He walked the earth performing miracles, He put together a team of men and trained them through His words and deeds. He would often share short stories with his disciples and the crowds who followed Him, and those short stories were packed with great meaning. In Luke 14:25-34, Jesus took time to explain to His disciples what "walking with God" entailed.

> Large crowds were traveling with Jesus and turning to them. He said: "If anyone comes to me and does not hate father and mother, wife and children, brothers, and sisters—yes, even their own life— such a person cannot be my disciple. And

whoever does not carry their cross and follow me cannot be my disciple. Suppose one of you wants to build a tower. Won't you first sit down and estimate the cost to see if you have enough money to complete it? For if you lay the foundation and are not able to finish it, everyone who sees it will ridicule you, saying, 'This person began to build and wasn't able to finish. Or suppose a king is about to go to war against another king. Won't he first sit down and consider whether he is able with ten thousand men to oppose the one coming against him with twenty thousand? If he is not able, he will send a delegation while the other is still a long way off and will ask for terms of peace. In the same way, those of you who do not give up everything you have cannot be my disciples."

Simply put, a wise person creates a strategy and a plan while also considering the cost of a project. Without a budget, a plan, and a strategy, a foolish person may find themselves in the project without the resources to complete it. When choosing to follow Christ, we must weigh the costs and consider if we are willing to let go of our will and desires for God's better. The same applies to choosing to abstain from sex until marriage. When I said yes to God regarding abstinence, and no to sex, I didn't weigh the cost of my decision. I didn't think that choice would end my long-term relationship; I thought that we would somehow work it out, but we didn't. Thus, abstinence became a long journey filled with complexities, blessings, struggles, triumphs, and lows. Although I am about eight or so years into this journey, I am completely satisfied with my decision.

I am an advocate for abstinence, and I understand that the choice is not an easy one to make. Our world is over-sexualized, and sex is used to market almost anything. Images of sex flash before our eyes through the media consistently and you can't get away from it even if you try. Our senses are easily aroused and charged by half-naked, 6-pack-carrying, chocolate-skinned men on Instagram.

With easy access to sex and the companionship that often accompanies it; why would anyone decide to be abstinent? It is not an easy ask and I consider all this whenever I speak about it. I also understand that although the Bible stresses that we shouldn't engage in sexual immorality, the reality is that this charge is not always enough for some. My recommendation for anyone who is thinking about leaping into waiting until marriage to have sex is, always build a relationship with God, because He is the best accountability partner on this journey. He can get your heart in check while giving you discernment on who and who not to give your heart to.

We obey God by obeying His word and what He says about pre-marital sex. Now while this is the "right" thing to do because God said so, there are other benefits of this decision.

Once you remove sex as an option in prospective relationships, you weed out who is for you and who is not. When my ex and I mutually decided to end our relationship, it showed me how much he valued sex over me and marriage. While this reality hurt, as I've already shared with you, it brought me clarity about who I was dating.

When you take sex off the table, you will see who will stick around with you. Any man after God's heart desires what God desires. If the fear of not having sex scares him, this is a great revelation for you! You will be able to see what he values. You don't need God to remove these men for you, they will do it themselves. It may hurt in the beginning, but hindsight will show you that it wasn't worth it. It's never worth it to be with someone who isn't committed to living for God.

Removing sex as an option also helps you to hear clearly. Let me explain. Before Christ, I was a hot-on-the-scene kinda girl! I was the girl who probably thought about sex more than men did. At least, so I thought. When I met someone new, my first thought was often, "I wonder what he's like in bed." I've known for so long that this thought process was most likely linked to my childhood trauma. There was very little "getting to know someone," I just didn't care. But when *I* decided to become abstinent, I had no other choice. I had no choice but to sit, listen, and ask a lot of questions. I've learned a lot about men and myself during this journey.

When you aren't having sex, you have to find other things to occupy your time. It was a catch-22 for me when I decided to abstain from sex. Again, I didn't think that I would be single for so long.

On one hand, it felt good to live for God, but on the other hand, I hated being alone sometimes. If God would have told me that my choice would lead to years of being single, to be frank, I probably wouldn't have done it. But just like a gentleman, God gently led me on this journey and opened up my eyes along the way. With so much free time on my hands, I've been able to identify my purpose, travel the world, build my brand, and heal! When Paul talks about singleness as a time to work for the Lord and not to worry about the cares of your spouse, this is what he means.

Now getting back to my decision to abstain from sex. When I reached a crossroads and had to decide on whether to stay in my relationship with my ex-boyfriend or to chase after God, I considered the cost. I could continue having pre-marital sex and get ordinary blessings or let the relationship go and receive the very best that God had for me. The beauty of a relationship with God is that He gives us free will to choose, and our choices lead us into the perfect will of His permissive will.

God's perfect will can be found throughout many stories in the bible but for the definition of perfect will, we can look to Romans.

> Do not conform to the pattern of this world, but be transformed by the renewing of your mind. Then you will be able to test and approve what God's will is—his good, pleasing, and **perfect will.** (Romans 12: 2)

From here, we can deduce that God has a perfect will that we can discern when we renew our minds. His perfect will is in complete opposition to what the world portrays as good. It doesn't take a magnifying glass to see what the patterns of this world are. Everything revolves around "sex, money, and drugs," and you can never get enough of it. God's perfect will was for Adam and Eve to enjoy all that He provided for them in the garden except the fruit from the Tree of Good and Evil. It was God's perfect will that man obeyed Him and enjoyed the riches that He provides. They decided that what God provided was not enough, so they ate from the Tree of Life, and sin (disobedience and separation from God) entered the world. This one choice is where the genesis of sin was formed. Do you think in God's perfect will He wanted us to be separated from Him? Absolutely not, but He allowed it. He allowed free will. This freedom of choice that Adam and Evil had in the garden is the same free will we have today. We have a choice on whether to test and approve what God's perfect will is and whether to oblige or not. I don't know about you, but I don't want to miss out on God's perfect will if I have a choice.

Can we go a bit deeper into God's permissive will versus His perfect will?

In 2 Timothy 2:20, the Bible teaches about a wealthy home filled with both wooden and gold utensils. The gold utensils were reserved for special use and the wooden and clay utensils were for everyday use. "In a wealthy home, there are dishes made of gold and silver as well as some made from wood and clay. The expensive dishes are used for guests, and the cheap ones are used in the kitchen or to put garbage in. If you stay away from sin, you will be like one of these dishes made of purest gold—the very best in the house—so that Christ himself can use you for his highest purposes."

I believe choosing God is perfectly illustrated by this scripture in 2 Timothy. God has put great purpose and potential in all of us. He has given us skills, talents, and abilities to do supernatural things here on earth. If you want to be used by God, at your fullest potential, you must be willing to present your body to Him as a living sacrifice; this is God's perfect will.

> "And so, dear brothers and sisters, I plead with you to give your bodies to God because of all he has done for you. Let them be a living and holy sacrifice–the kind he will find acceptable. This is truly the way to worship him." (Romans 12:1 NLT)

God desires to use a pure and willing vessel. If we want supernatural things from God and if we want doors to open, we have to be willing to sacrifice ourselves to receive them. This goes for women as much as it does for men. Women are not the only ones called to carry the burden of waiting until marriage for sex.

If we decide to follow our own desires, we will fall into God's permissive will, what God allows. It is our choice as to whether we want to be like the wood and clay utensils and used naturally or like the gold utensils and used supernaturally. There are things that we want to do, in our minds, but our motives lie in our hearts, and these motives push us to make choices. Are you willing to let pre-marital sex hinder you from God's abundant blessings? Obedience proves to God that you are ready for greater work. God wants to trust you with what He has for you. Celibacy and the choosing purity is not just about a sex choice; it's a life choice. If you can be faithful over your body, God can trust you to be faithful with the blessings He has for you, because "someone has been given much, much will be required in return; and when someone has been entrusted with much, more will be required." (Luke 12:48 NLT)

God's will regarding sex can be found in 1 Thessalonians 4:3, and his will is for us to be sanctified, and avoid sexual immorality in order to access everything He has for us. His thoughts about us are good and He wills to give us hope and a future. (Jeremiah 29:11).

God's will is also expressed in the book of Hebrews.

> "Now may the God of peace, who through
> the blood of the eternal covenant
> brought back from the dead our Lord

Jesus, that great Shepherd of the sheep,
equip you with everything good for doing
his will, and may he work in us what is
pleasing to him, through Jesus Christ, to
whom be glory forever and ever. Amen."
(Hebrews 13:20-21)

God wants to give us great blessings, but we
must come in alignment with His perfect will for us. We
can have a good life in His permissive will, and an
amazing one in His perfect will.

Entering God's perfect will does not mean our
choices will be perfect. Choosing to abstain from sex
indicates our heart is chasing after purity, but purity
does not mean perfect. I accept that I am not perfect,
and I will make mistakes, and I did make mistakes. I
remember a time when I broke my vow of celibacy; it
was two years after I ended my long-term relationship
and made the choice to be abstinent.

A friend invited me out to a club in Manhattan.
Everything in me cautioned me against going and I
remember dragging my feet to get dressed because The
Holy Spirit wanted me to stay home. I went anyway,
and even though it had been a while since I'd partied,
not much had changed. The atmosphere was dark, the
music was blaring, and I could feel the thickness of lust
in the atmosphere. I approached the bar, and a young

man approached me. We exchanged words and then telephone numbers. There was something quite familiar about him, but I picked up on something that I had come in contact with before that I couldn't quite pinpoint. He had a familiar mysteriousness about him. When he inquired if my friend and I could use a ride home, I, against my better judgment, obliged.

After dropping my friend off at home, he took me home. This stranger and I established no clear boundaries and, as a result, it was easy for me to break my vow of celibacy. Later that evening, while on the phone with him, I could barely understand him, I kept asking him to repeat himself over and over again. Out of frustration, I hung up the phone. Then I lay in my bed as the memories of our time together replayed in my head, leaving me feeling ashamed and confused.

The word of God says that "God is spirit, and his worshipers must worship Him in the Spirit and truth." So let me tell you the truth because I know some of you are wondering, "why would you let a stranger drive you home?" The truth is I've always been the adventurous type.

When God enters your life, He doesn't change your personality, He changes your character. Before I was saved, my sex drive was very high. Remember, I knew no boundaries when it came to sex. In that moment of temptation, I was led away by my own desires, lack of self-control, and lust.

The following day was Sunday; I woke up, got dressed, and reluctantly dragged myself to church. With the weight of my mistake weighing heavily on my shoulders, I was stuck on why I couldn't understand him. Immediately, I heard the voice of God say, "My sheep know my voice, and a stranger's voice they will not follow."

When he has brought out all his own, he goes on ahead of them, and his sheep follow him because they know his voice. But they will never follow a stranger; in fact, they will run away from him because they do not recognize a stranger's voice." (John 10:4-5 NIV)

That's when the tears began to fall, and the shame and regret were lifted immediately. I'd made a mistake, and I had created a bond with another man who was not my husband and it left me feeling ashamed. Sex with him was not *just* a fun pastime, and a cycle of sexual encounters with men that left me feeling empty like the Samaritan woman was my story. However, I knew God was with me. What I would later learn was that because I desired marriage, every sexual encounter I had with a man who was not my husband, would inevitably lead to disappointment. Days after having sex with this man, I decided to put on my CIA suit. After digging for hours, I finally came across a tagged photo of him by his wife on FB. I felt disgusted but thankful that God is both powerful and forgiving.

That experience was a turning point in my abstinence journey. I realized that if I was to take this walk seriously, I couldn't do it without God.

Abstinence is not only a head decision but also a heart choice. Your mind and heart must agree that this is something you desire to do. If you are simply abstaining from sex because you "know" it's God's will for you; that will only get you but so far. When the knowledge travels to your heart, then you can commit to doing it.

Don't do what the word says is correct just because you read it, let your heart come into agreement with it. This is the difference between religion and relationships. Religion says, "because the Bible says we shouldn't have sex before marriage, I won't." Relationships say, "because I want to please God and get the best He has for me, I won't."

For the two years before my slip-up, I'd been practicing abstinence from a religious standpoint. I knew what the word of God said concerning me and I remembered His promise to me in Deuteronomy 28. I was wearing my abstinence as a badge of honor of some sort. I beat myself into obedience without truly understanding my choice apart from it "being the right thing to do." At the moment when I slipped up, I realized that I didn't want that pain anymore. I didn't want a relationship built from sex alone. I no longer wanted to give my body to a man that wasn't my husband. I no longer found value in that. It wasn't doing it for me anymore.

At that moment, I told God: "Anything I do for you, I want to come from my heart."

The thought of being abstinent can seem like a daunting and impossible task when we approach it with a getting-it-perfect mindset. The thought of making mistakes in abstinence often hinders many from making the choice. Some often wait until they know that they will be able to be abstinent without slipping up. The waiting-to-become-perfect moment never comes and the choice to live free and in God's will is often missed. "How am I going to give up sex for a certain amount of time?" is a question I hear a lot, and one I often ask myself. Here's the key to it all, you don't try to do it without God.

In my weak moments, I can accept that I am human with limited power and that God has unlimited power. Purity and celibacy do not mean perfect. You will slip up and make mistakes; don't let the thought of this overtake you and hinder you from choosing to be abstinent. I don't walk around with a picket sign encouraging everyone to be abstinent because celibacy is a heart choice, not a mental choice. Don't choose based on what you think you can't do but rather on what God can equip you to do. God's word says that when we are weak or tempted, we can find strength in God. Our weaknesses show us just how strong and powerful God truly is. I couldn't have fathomed the thought of giving up sex for this long, but it was through the grace of God. I was reassured in my decision to wait because He said, "My grace is sufficient for you, for my power is made perfect in weakness. Therefore I will boast all the more gladly about my weaknesses, so that Christ's power may rest on me. That is why, for Christ's sake, I delight in weaknesses, insults, hardships, persecutions, and difficulties. For when I am weak, then I am strong."

Let God do the work in and through you.

REFLECTION

God doesn't force anything on us, which means that giving up sex until marriage is a choice. He lays His desires out before us in His word coupled with the benefits of obeying and the reality of what happens if you don't. But let's face it, not having sex is not natural. Unless you have been blessed with the gift of celibacy, which Paul talks about in Corinthians, giving up sex is not an easy feat. The Holy Spirit is what empowers us to do what we don't have the natural tendency to do. In our heads, we may know what God's will is and do it but the desire to please God rests in our hearts. Luke 6:45 says: "A good man out of the good treasure of his heart bringeth forth that which is good; and an evil man out of the evil treasure of his heart bringeth forth that which is evil: for of the abundance of the heart his mouth speaketh." Our hearts hold our true treasures (desires). I am no stranger to mistakes; my abstinence walk has not been perfect. But it is through my slip-ups and setbacks that I've learned what it truly means to carry my cross and I don't have to do it alone. Neither do you.

Deciding to follow what God's word says regarding sex before marriage is really up to you. God is not going to twist your hand, and neither am I. I want to simply offer you another perspective and a better way. I say that with love for you and hope for your future.

Are you committed to making the choice today to say no to sex and yes to God? Are you ready to pick up your cross and chase Him? The choice is yours.

LET'S PRAY

Gracious God, I come before you now lifting up the sister reading this who may be struggling to abstain from sex. I pray that Your Spirit will lead her into fellowship with you. I pray that as your mature her through experiences and circumstances she will know your love. I pray that you will give her insight and discernment regarding your will for her. I pray that she will come to understand that she cannot do anything apart from you. Convict her heart to say yes to you and deliver her from the shame of her past or mistakes that may cause her to drift from you.

I pray that you will stir up in her the fire to chase after you in obedience. You say, " Your word I have hidden in my heart that I might not sin against you." May your word rest in her heart today.

In Jesus' name. Amen.

16.

Spiritual Warfare is Real

In the song, "Freedom Time," Lauryn Hill, pens the words:

> "Yo, there's a war in the mind, over territory
>
> For the dominion
>
> Who will dominate the opinion"?

The song paints a picture of the spiritual battle that goes on in our minds. We live in an age where we are flooded with -ologies and opinions. We are constantly thrown images of what we should and shouldn't think. We may often feel a tug or pull in many different directions. The world and the media want us to believe and desire things that are usually different and opposite from what is good for us! This, my friends, is an example of what spiritual warfare looks like.

As believers, we have to understand that our enemy is Satan. Thousands of years before you and I came to earth, Satan rebelled against God. He rebelled because he wanted to be like God. What did God do? He gave Satan the power to rule the earth.

> If the Good News we preach is hidden behind a veil, it is hidden only from people who are perishing. Satan, who is the god of this world, has blinded the minds of those who don't believe. They are unable to see the glorious light of the Good News. They don't understand this message about the glory of Christ, who is the exact likeness of God. (2 Corinthians 4:3-4 NLT)

If Satan is the god of this world and can blind the minds of those who don't believe, then we can easily deduce that he has power. Power is defined as the ability to do something according to the Merriam-Webster dictionary. If he has the power to blind those who don't believe, do you think that he is not exercising that? Of course, he is. Satan knows that his time here to rule on the earth is short. At the end of time, Jesus will be victorious and banish Satan to his home, hell.

Because of this fact, Satan is consistently seeking to take people with him. He does this by attacking our minds with lies about our identity, our purposes, and the character of God. Think of your mind as a territory; Satan is after dominion over this territory. He gains dominion through a war that you fight. For this reason, God instructs us to put on the full armor of the Lord so that we can stand against the wiles (schemes) of Satan. God also encourages us that the weapons of our warfare are not carnal (physical) but rather spiritual. This means that if we are to fight against Satan, we are not doing so with physical tools but rather spiritual weaponry.

Now that we have a little more clarity on my take on spiritual warfare, let's get into the war on lust.

Ten years ago, I accepted Jesus Christ as my Lord and Savior. I have been attending church for the same amount of time. A decade after choosing Christ, I have come to realize that many of the challenges I have had in life are completely overlooked by the church, some intentionally and others ignorantly. One of my goals for this book is not only to challenge what you know but also what you have believed by addressing some topics the church does not address. As earlier expressed, many churches are not willing to address the issues of sex from the pulpit, and this leaves us to figure things out on our own.

Fortunately, some of us partner with God and the Holy Spirit to lead us to a true understanding. Unfortunately, many are misled, misdirected, and have to unlearn a lot. Alongside sex, spiritual warfare is prevalent in our everyday lives but completely overlooked in the western church. It would be irresponsible to share my natural experiences in my season of singleness and neglect the spiritual experiences that occurred. For many, this may be new knowledge, and my goal is to share with you as much as I know, in hopes that you take this information to God in prayer and google for research.

According to Ephesians 6:12, we are not only influenced by what we naturally see as temptations but there are also dark forces in operation that we cannot see with our naked eye. If we believe in God whom we cannot see, then we can believe that there is a lower power operating to which we are naturally blind. Since the beginning of time, Satan has been attempting to turn the hearts of men away from God and to him.

Satan was kicked out of heaven because he wanted to take God's glory. He wanted to be worshipped over God. The Bible tells us that Satan was kicked out of heaven to roam the earth. From reading the Bible, we also learn that Satan is the god of this world which simply means that he has the power to rule the earth through influences called principalities, and spiritual wickedness in high places. These forces are, at the least, in opposition to God's will being manifested in your life. So what are these principalities concerning us and how do they interact with us on our road to marriage.

Since the Garden of Eden, Satan has planned to deceive man by offering us things that satisfy our flesh (the natural side of us). Our flesh desires to do everything opposite of God, this does not make us "bad" but rather it shows us our humanity. God understands the temptations that this world is filled with, hence he instructed Adam and Eve not to eat from the Tree of Life, giving in to the lust of the eye to satisfy a natural need.

Of course, they disobeyed God, ate from the tree, and introduced sin into the world. Sin is separation from God. When Satan was thrown out of heaven, he was cast down to be eternally separated from God. This would have been destiny but thank God for Jesus. God desires and gives us access to Him when we accept Jesus as our Lord and Savior. However, Satan wants company, and he will continue to tempt us to sin and keep us separated from God. He doesn't rest in his attempts to sabotage our relationship with the Father, and this is the simple basis of spiritual warfare.

The temptation to sin is a form of spiritual warfare because the devil uses the various options of available sin to whisper lies to us about God and us. An example of spiritual warfare is found in Jesus' temptation in the wilderness.

In Matthew 4, Satan tempted Jesus after a 40-day fast. Jesus was not only God, but He was fully man as well and had the same natural desires we have. Jesus was hungry. Satan tempted Jesus with something that he knew would satisfy Jesus' flesh, food. Satan appeared and offered Jesus food if Jesus would sin and give in to his demands. Food satisfies our flesh just like sex.

Spiritual warfare is also often launched against our purpose, destiny, and what God says about us, and the story of Job illustrates this perfectly. Satan expressed to God that he had been going back and forth on the earth looking for a moment to attack us, our purpose, and our destiny. He chose Job and attacked and destroyed life as Job knew it. He didn't stop there; he also attacked his mindset and belief about who God is and what God says.

If God has promised you that you will wed, as His word says, and your marriage is purposeful, as His word says, why wouldn't the enemy want to hinder that? The adversary cannot force you to do anything, and neither can God, we have been given the gift of free will. However, **we can be tempted to abandon our destiny and God's purposes for us when we take heed to the lies of Satan.** Satan tries to block the plans of God for our lives by bombarding us with false accusations, and I have had to choose to disregard them regardless of how truthful they sound.

The enemy tried this in late 2020 when I lost my aunt, Renee. She was the woman who took me in as a child and raised me on her own. I will explore the story of how she passed in another book, however, there is an important lesson I learned about Satan and his attack after she passed.

While she was sick, I prayed that God would heal her, and God did not answer my prayers. The unexpected passing of my aunt left me with a bitter heart towards God. Not only did I feel as though God had let me down, but I questioned my identity and calling in Christ.

For so long, I have known and believed that God speaks to me. As a prophet of God, my call is to hear from God and share what He says. When I prayed to God to save my aunt, I heard him say that she would not die; at least, that's what I believe I heard. When my aunt passed away, it made me question everything. I questioned whether or not I had ever heard God before. And I questioned my identity and my purpose.

The enemy does not play, he never does. He whispered lies to me about my purpose, my identity, and my standing with God. "You don't hear God." "Look, he let your aunt die. God doesn't answer your prayers." "Look at all the things you've waited on God to do that he hasn't done yet." "God will never come through for you."

These lies and accusations from Satan about my identity turned into lies and accusations about my singleness. "Look, you're still single." "Everyone else is married except for you." "Look how long you've been waiting; God isn't going to come through on His promises to you." "What's the use of being abstinent, you might as well just have sex." These are all the lies the adversary threw at me. We often minimize these phrases to our thoughts, but we need to be able to distinguish between our voice, God's, and the enemy's.

If you are truly desiring a spouse and have not yet attained it, this may cause you to doubt that God can provide you with one. Maybe you too have been plagued by the words that Satan whispered to me during my season of vulnerability.

You need to put on your armor. And just like any war, you must be prepared with the right arsenal of weapons and strategy! Ephesians 6:10 - 18 lists these 5 weapons we must use in any fight against the enemy: the belt of truth, the breastplate of righteousness, the gospel of peace, the shield of faith, the helmet of salvation, and prayer.

For me to fight against these seeds of deception that the enemy threw my way, I had to put on my armor every day. I want to show you how you can do the same in your daily war against Satan over your mind.

The Belt of Truth

The truth is the word of God and a belt holds everything up. Understanding and applying the word of God is what will hold you together when you feel things are falling apart.

An example of applying the word of truth is saying: Dear God, I know what you say about me. I understand what you have said to me in Your Word. You say, I am the head and not the tail. You say that I am fearfully and wonderfully made. You've spoken and said that I am not forgotten or overlooked, you will leave the ninety-nine to reach me. You give me the desires of my heart, according to your word. You have given me the desire to wed. I am not wrong for feeling this way. As you have placed this desire in my heart, I trust that you will fulfill it. I stand on this truth, and I apply it to my mind right now in Jesus' name.

The Breastplate of Righteousness

To be righteous is to live your life for God. A breastplate is a device used to protect your heart. If your heart is where your desires are, wouldn't it be important to keep it covered (protected from being attacked)? Living righteous and monitoring your desires may look like setting aside your own desires and will and choosing what God wants for you. This may also look like fleeing from self-indulgence or anything that would cause you to be separated from God.

The bible doesn't explicitly say anything about masturbation however, this is clearly a self-indulgent act.

When I gave up sex, I also gave up pornography and masturbation because they were obstacles for me. In my attempt to keep my commitment to God, I denied myself self-gratifying things.

This is a daily task as we try to be more like Christ, something I don't hear talked about often.

A prayer to put on the armor of God can be: Lord, I desire to please you. I put on the breastplate of righteousness right now. I set aside my self-indulgent and self-gratifying pleasures and I take up my cross to chase you. You desire the very best for me. I trust your will over mine. Help me to find comfort in what I have been given in this season. Help me to set aside my insatiable desire to want more. Lord, give me the self-control and discipline to cease doing anything that doesn't please you. Guard my heart now in Jesus' name. Amen.

The Gospel of Peace

The gospel is simple: Jesus Christ was crucified, died, buried, and rose from the grave. He did so to give us the ability to repent (turn from sin) and access eternity with Him. Jesus walked the earth and preached the message of his pending death and resurrection. It was a message of peace. The Gospel gives you access to God.

> Jesus answered, "I am the way and the truth and the life. No one comes to the Father except through me. (John 14:6 NIV)

The best relationship you will ever have is one with God and the way to God is through Jesus. As a single woman, I had to acknowledge and accept this as truth. The love of God pales in comparison to any form of human love. As you are putting on the gospel of peace, you are remembering Christ's sacrifice for you. Remember that you are free because of His love for you. You do not have to be victim to the lies of the enemy. You have access to God's redeeming love. Let's put on the gospel of peace: Dear God, thank you for sending your only son to die on the cross for my sins. The wages of my sin was death, but you pardoned me because of your sacrifice. Regardless of the lies the enemy tries to fill my mind with, I know that I am loved and valued. I stand affirmed in that truth.

The Shield of Faith

The enemy will try to attack your faith in God to provide you with a spouse. He will try to make it seem as if you will never be married. You may have spent years comparing yourself to everyone else who is. This only leaves you feeling more doubtful and burdened. Now, some married folks may say: don't focus on marriage, just focus on yourself. I would love to take a peek into their past and see how they handled their singleness. I digress. I understand what it feels like to desire marriage and there's nothing wrong with this. If God's promised you a spouse, you can rest assured of two things:

1. God cannot lie. If He made a promise to you, He will manifest it in your life.
2. The enemy will attack your belief system. He fights us in the areas where we are vulnerable. Read John 10:10, he is a roaring lion seeking whom he may devour. Think about the nature of a lion. It waits patiently to attack when its victim is the most vulnerable. The enemy is waiting to catch you slipping.

With this knowledge, I'm sure you understand why it is important to put on the shield of faith. The shield protects your heart (your value). Let's put on the shield of faith: Heavenly Father, you said that all we need is a mustard seed size faith to move mountains. You are not requiring much from us. You know the areas where we struggle to believe, thank you for meeting us there. Today, I put on the shield of faith and I stand firm on your truth. I believe by faith that you will provide me with the desires that you have placed in my heart. I thank you in advance for my purpose mate. Thank you for aligning our paths. Thank you for giving me the endurance to wait until you have decided it is time for us to meet.

In Jesus' name, I pray. Amen.

The Helmet of Salvation

We are saved once we repent and accept Jesus as Our Lord and Savior. I gave my life to God over 10 years ago and if I could be honest, things became mundane. I knew that I was saved but I lost the excitement and fire for God. When spiritual battles began to intensify, I started to reclaim my identity, the fire began to burn again. I took refuge in the hope that I was already victorious over the schemes of the enemy because of my salvation. I knew I was victorious, and I started to operate from this perspective in my prayer life. There comes a point on your journey where you will get tired of the enemy sifting you like wheat. If you fight enough in one area you will eventually, hopefully, start to fight back. You must fight from a place of victory. You have already had every battle against Satan, and He has no authority over you or your future. When the enemy begins to plant seeds of doubt about your identity, who you belong to, your worth, and your future; you can combat them by putting on the helmet of salvation.

The Sword of the Spirit

One of my favorite pieces of armor to put on is the sword of the spirit which is the word of God. The bible is alive and active which Is why a verse today can have a completely different meaning to you months from now. In the word of God, you will find help and wisdom for every question or issue you have.

There is a scripture you can assign to every single challenge you are facing right now. As believers, it is imperative that we not only read the word of God but apply it to our lives. What are you struggling with right now in your single season? Is it doubt? Low self-worth? Abandonment? Rejection? Shame? Find a scripture that you can memorize and repeat in order to renew your mind. Joyce Meyers authored a book called " The Battlefield of The Mind, and according to the book, our mind is the place where we fight the enemy. It's time for you to fight back with the sword. The sword will spiritually cut through every lie you have believed about yourself.

Let's go: Dear God, thank you for giving me access to all of these power tools for warfare. You don't leave me ill-equipped. Thank you for the helmet of salvation that I put on right now as I remember that I'm victorious. You have given me victory over every lie of the enemy about my identity and your promises to me. Thank you for this reminder today.

How to hear from God

One of the most common questions people ask me is, how do you hear from God? Here are three ways that you can hear from God. I am sharing this with you because as single women, we need to partner with God on our journey. The only way you are going to partner with God is to be able to discern and follow His voice. This singleness is not a time to journey aimlessly, it's a grace period. It's a time in between God's promises. So let's buckle down and refine our ears to hear him now because you need to be able to discern a counterfeit from the real thing, amongst other things.

Here are three ways you can hear from God:

Time + Intimacy

If your close friend calls you from a strange number and you pick up, you will know it's them, right? Why? Because you spend time with them. The more you speak to an individual the more you become accustomed to their voice. This is no different than God. When you first begin to spend time with God it may seem strange. You're picturing it now; there you are alone in your room sitting in silence listening for this loud audible voice. Throw that image away right now.

Spending time with God is simply allowing God space in your day and your life. It can be as simple as a morning prayer to start the day or a mid-day 'thank you, Lord.' Start getting accustomed to walking with the Lord. Remember, you are never alone, God is always with you even when you don't feel it. The more you accept that truth, spending time with God will not be a foreign concept to you.

Reading God's Word

The easiest way to discern your voice from the enemy's and God's voice is to read the word of God. God's nature and character are written throughout the 66 books of the bible. The Bible gives you clear illustrations of how God interacts with His people. The promises of God are found throughout His word. If what you hear doesn't line up with God's nature or

God's promises, this is a sure-fire way to discern that it's not from God.

Prayer

James 1:5 says, If any of you lacks wisdom, let him ask of God, that giveth to all men liberally, and upbraideth not; and it shall be given him. What an amazing Father God is that He invites us into communion with Him. If you desire to hear God, ask Him to help refine your ear. God desires to hear from you. He has a lot to say and He wants to give you the wisdom to discern His voice.

Being able to discern God's voice has helped me on my journey of abstinence and singleness. A few years ago, I had a dream that I was taking a shower with a man I did not know. Another man was in the bathroom watching us and he was quite jealous that I was with this man and not him. He glared at me as I showered with his friend. The friend tried to get me to have sex with him, but I decided not to.

Keep in mind, I did not know these men nor have I ever seen their faces. After we got out of the shower, we entered a room and it happened to be my father's old bedroom. In the room, the gentleman I showered with is now sitting on the bed getting dressed. He looks at me and says, "you're not going to go crazy like the other women right? Like calling and harassing me. What happened tonight was nothing." I looked at him confused and replied, "No, I'm not like that." At that point, I felt enticed into having sex with him and I did. As he penetrated me in the dream, I woke up.

It was a lucid dream, and I still felt the sensation as I arose that morning.

Why would God allow me to have a sex dream?

Is this God testing me or is this the enemy tempting me?

We know from scripture that God does not lead us, encourage us, or tempt us to sin. "When tempted, no one should say, "God is tempting me." For God cannot be tempted by evil, nor does he tempt anyone." (James 1:13)

Fighting the War on Lust

Something or someone led me to have sex with the gentleman in my dream, and if it wasn't God, then who was it? Satan, of course. No other powers are working apart from God but evil. The tricky part to all this is the notion and truth that although God doesn't tempt us to do wrong, He allows Satan to do so. How then do we reconcile sexual dreams?

I thought back to my day-to-day actions and leaned into what may have evoked that sexual dream. Before this particular dream, I hadn't had a sexual dream in over a year. After forgiving my ex-boyfriend, the dreams between me and him stopped so what was this? The only thing that changed in my day-to-day activities was that I had started watching TV and more movies that were not faith-based. Some have looked at me as weird or lame when I've told them, in times past, that I didn't watch television. I was very disciplined in this area because I knew how women, children, and sex are exploited on television. Now, these are the things that we all know (at least I would hope). What's the harm in all of this you think?

As I started indulging in more television, I noticed how television had become less censored. What used to be innuendos of sex behind closed doors were now full-out nudity and on-air sex scenes. I remember when sex was left to the imagination, and these seeds and suggestions weren't being planted. We have to be mindful of what we are consuming, it all matters.

After the dream, I had to partner with God so that I wouldn't desire to feel that penetration that I felt in the dream, in real life. Part of winning the war is being aware of your triggers and the things you allow in your life and mind. It is one thing to fight against the lies of the enemy when he attacks your purpose by purporting lies, and it is another to willingly let him in by the choices you make in your daily life.

Another level of the spiritual battle that we engage in is one that you can attest to if you live in America; that is the battle against lust. Because we live in a sex-pumped world, and because sex is in everything, it is a kind of warfare many of us are engaged in.

When I decided to give up sex until marriage as a vow to God in 2013, it was because I didn't want to miss out on what God had for me. For years, I marched to this promise thinking that my decision was solely tied to my obedience to God's word in Deuteronomy 28. In 2020, seven years after, I realized that being abstinent was more than simply an act of obedience but what would free me from the spirit of lust.

> For we wrestle not against flesh and blood, but against principalities, against powers, against the rulers of the darkness of this world, against spiritual wickedness in high places. (Ephesians 6:12 KJV)

Lust is a strong craving or desire, often of a sexual nature. Lust is not an action but rather a spirit that can lead to actions that will cause us to fall into sexual sin. I battled with the spirit of lust for many years.

What makes lust different from our natural desire for sex is that it controls us and is insatiable, it is never satisfied.

In my earlier years, I could not look at a man without desiring to have sex with him or imagining what sex with him would be like. I thought this was a natural desire until I found myself wrapped up in multiple sexual partners left empty and unfulfilled.

We feed the spirit of lust when we entertain it through vain imaginations, participating in sexual acts, pornography, and masturbation. Lust will control you because it is never satisfied. Abstinence isn't what broke the spirit of lust off of me, but it helped me to stop feeding it so that I could get my inner healing from God.

We must cut it at the root by addressing and attacking it with the word of God, prayer, and fasting.

However, there are other practical steps you need to take like setting clear boundaries and getting accountability partners in the war against lust, or else it will be impossible to break free of its destructive effects

Set Clear Boundaries

Boundaries are necessary! I don't know how much I can stress their importance. I have boundaries in some areas and a lot of discipline in others – but I need help with self-control; see, I lack in this area. I can be honest with myself. Establishing boundaries is what has helped me to not fall into sin. We are called to live in this world but not to be wrongly influenced by it!

This is a hard task to achieve, trust me, I know! You know God is aware that we will be tempted right? You didn't think He was unaware of the temptations we face as single women, did you? You can be reassured that God knows all about temptation because His word says:

"The temptations in your life are no different from what others experience" (1 Corinthians 10:13a. NLT)

You are in good company.

God tells us that even though we are tempted, He has a plan for us to overcome temptations; it's called "A Way Out." God's escape for us is this:

"He will not allow the temptation to be more than you can stand. When you are tempted, he will show you a way out so that you can endure." (1 Corinthians 10:13b NLT)

Sis, you can't tell me that before you did something with someone you didn't think about your actions over a million times in your head! I think we all had this conversation with ourselves: "I really shouldn't call him," "I should block his number," and "I probably shouldn't text him back."

Do we listen to the escape plans that God gives us or the boundaries he has repeatedly asked us to set? Sometimes, no. That internal conversation that we have with ourselves is our escape route. Have you ever been in the heat of the moment with someone and something totally out of the ordinary happens, something so weird you can't deny it? That's your way out.

When God says He will give us an escape route, this is what He is talking about. If you are trying to maintain an abstinent lifestyle, there are certain things you shouldn't do if you know it's going to jeopardize your celibacy. For example no late-night visits in intimate settings. Why would I set myself up like that? I think some people get the idea that once you're abstinent, you lose your desire to have sex...wrong. The desire is present which is why discipline and sacrifice are so important.

So what do I do to set boundaries and fight temptations? I don't place myself in situations where I know I will be tempted. Let's say, for instance, that I go on a date with a really good-looking guy, no nightcaps are happening afterward. I am not coming over for Netflix and chill. I may also have to avoid going out too late if I can't handle my sex drive. Okay, maybe I took things too far. But what I mean is that you know your level of self-control! I have to control myself to have self-control. To do that, I stopped placing myself in situations where I know I will be tempted to engage in something that will break my vow of celibacy to God. You too have to exercise the same wisdom when dating if you chose to be abstinent.

Another thing that I started to practice that is often overlooked is this: I stopped having late-night conversations. This is a boundary that you should set for yourself as well. It's easy for seeds to be planted when it's late at night and your guards are down. During the wee hours of the night, a guy can tell you anything and you may believe it.

It took me a long time, but I had to realize that I could no longer entertain men with whom I saw no future. When you meet a guy for the first time, you are almost certain whether he is someone you can see yourself with. If your goal is marriage, you don't have time to waste entertaining men who you cannot envision spending your life with. If you're anything like me, this is hard to accept because you fall into that percentage of women who think they can change men. Women are created to create, so we naturally have a desire to mold, shape, and nurture. However, you cannot save a man! You cannot mold and shape a man into who you want him to be. You cannot make a man more honest, more genuine, more righteous, or more into you; that's God's work. You can't make a man a husband.

The best practice I've found, with dating and celibacy that I cannot stress enough is to always present my relationship to God first. When you allow God into your relationships, you allow Him to close every door of distraction that comes in the form of a man.

Stop entertaining prospects. Seek God on whether the man is truly for you and if not, close the door and run in the opposite direction. Having that one-night stand after two years of celibacy was not the first or last time that I was tempted to sin. Through countless temptations, I truly learned what it means to *"Submit yourselves, then, to God,"* and I stopped trying to *"Resist the devil and temptation."* (James 4:7)

What are your triggers and what boundaries do you need to set in place to fight temptations?

Another way to set boundaries is around the kind of men you date. It is easier to implement boundaries when you stop ignoring the fruit! The word of God says you will know them by their fruit. Some of us feel we lack the ability to discern God's voice; this is something that I can understand. As mentioned earlier, the ability to understand God's voice is like a muscle that you must continue to work out.

However, you do not need discernment to recognize the fruit someone bears. You know an orange tree is an orange tree because it bears oranges. You will be able to distinguish orange trees from other fruit-bearing trees because of the fruits they bear. If you open your eyes, you can see clearly what's right in front of you. And, if you keep your eyes open; you will never be led astray. Am I at liberty to say this? We are never bamboozled, we just ignore the fruit (the signs, the red flags). So what are the fruits of the Spirit?

What are those obvious things that show you he ain't the one, Sis? Just because he has a scripture in his bio on Instagram does not mean he is a man of God. Does this man have integrity? Do his actions and his words align? If he claims to be a man of God, you must interrogate what his relationship to the word of God is.

What are his views on the things of God? What does he think about the nature of God? How does he treat his friends, family, and his mother? What is his response to change or challenges? Is he quick to anger?

Does he have patience? Is he long-suffering? Does he have a heart of service? Is he compassionate? Does he have mercy for those who are marginalized? Now, your values may differ from mine, however, the character and the nature of the man you desire to date should align with the nature of God.

REFLECTION

Get an Accountability Partner or Two

Some game shows on TV make this available to their contestants, as Christians, we should incorporate this into our lives.

"I'd like to use a lifeline."

"Which one would you like to use?"

"Can I phone a friend?"

Sis, aside from studying the word, taking this to God through prayer and fasting, and setting clear boundaries, you need a community to win spiritual battles.

Accountability partners are so necessary when trying to date God's way. They are there to remind you of who you are in Christ and to keep you focused on the end goal: mine is marriage and victory against lust and pre-marital sex.

They are there to say, "Sis, he ain't the one." They are there to help you flee in the moments when you want to fall.

A strong community of men and women will help you maintain your vow of celibacy and ultimately lead you to God's destiny for your life.

LET'S PRAY

Lord, I am coming to you today because I need your help. I acknowledge that I cannot do this on my own. As much as I want to be married, I want the best that you have for me. Help me to put my flesh under subjection and help me to fight these temptations that are ever so present. Your word says: "for every temptation, you give us a route of escape" so help me to make wise choices. Give me the wisdom to not only make better choices but the strength to follow through. Help me to cut ties with any man that is from my past or present that I know is a hindrance to me. Give me the faith to put my #relationshipgoals in your hands.

In Jesus's name. Amen.

17.

Dating with God

Dating while celibate is one of the hardest things I have had to do. I'd become more bitter and pessimistic about dating because of the experiences I'd had, and I held on to a lot of what happened to me and didn't often address my role in the situation.

If I can be honest with myself, I was very hopeful that the men I dated were "the one." Because I held those expectations, I probably didn't enjoy dating as much as I could have or should have. I would often hear people suggest to me that I needed to be free and date without having expectations, but that was hard for me to do.

It was hard because I often wondered if I would ever find an abstinent, God-fearing man with integrity and common sense. They were out there, but I didn't find that out until I had gone through a series of bad apples.

A few years after my slip up with abstinence, I found myself back out on the dating scene. This time, it was at a lounge. One night, while at my then-favorite dancing, nightspot, I introduced myself to this tall, dark chocolate, and handsome guy. I named him Mr. Hot Chocolate. We exchanged numbers and soon after went on a date.

On the first date, he was very much a gentleman and invited me to a company-sponsored jazz event. I remember him making a really good first impression and making me feel special, so I was open after that. For those who are not familiar with AAVE, I was very interested in him. Our second date was a tad more intimate than our first date; we went to eat at a lounge near his home.

One thing led to another, and I found myself sharing a very passionate kiss with him in a room off the lounge that happened to become empty. I knew my boundaries and was aware that the next step was sex for me, based on my last encounter.

This was how my mind operated. I knew no limits and, at this point, I was so deep in the moment that I couldn't think clearly. It had also been years since I'd been touched by a man and his initial touch ignited the fire in me.

At that moment, I told God that I was going to give in to the temptation. I sinned in my heart first.

Matthew 5:28 says,

> "But I tell you that anyone who looks at a woman lustfully has already committed adultery with her in his heart."

We think sin happens when we commit the act but here we see that even the thought is already sinning. I don't know about you, but once I commit to something, rarely will I not follow through.

In the case of Mr. Hot Chocolate, I had already decided that I was going to sleep with him or so I thought.

I was having numerous flashbacks to the first and last time I broke my vow of celibacy when suddenly, the Holy Spirit caught hold of me and I knew I didn't want to fall into the same trap as I had before. We left the lounge and I ignorantly followed him to the front of his apartment building where I had to fight off the temptation to follow him upstairs, even as he assured me that "nothing was going to happen."

Do you remember the old school movies where you see a devil on one shoulder and an angel on the other and the person on whose shoulders they're standing is forced to make a tough choice? Well, that is what it felt like to me.

My flesh said, "Go upstairs" and my spirit said, "Call a cab." "God help me," I finally uttered, subconsciously. Then just as soon as I said that I took out my phone and started to call for a cab. I allowed God into the situation! God helped me to resist the temptation because I didn't have the strength to do it on my own.

In the Bible, there are people called guardsmen, and their role was to guard the city walls because there were valuables inside the walls of the city. They weren't letting anything suspicious get past them, and they weren't ignoring the signs either.

Sis, you're valuable. The guards had to be alert at all times.

We must GUARD OUR HEARTS. You are a prized possession and so is your heart. Everyone doesn't deserve access to it! The same goes for you. You don't have to fall into temptation every time you are tempted. You can invite God into the situation and ask for his help, and He will give you a way out.

I found that these bad apples don't only exist on the physical dating scene in lounges and churches, but also online.

Six years into my singleness journey, I decided to be intentional about online dating. So I created a profile and joined the 30.4 million users of all the dating sites[1] and was ready to explore my options. Although God didn't lead me to try online dating, I can say that He used every experience and disappointment for my good and this book!

The first guy that I talked to on the dating app was about 5 years younger than me. He made it a point to mention that he was "mature for his age" which to me was a clear sign of immaturity. We talked for days on the app, which eventually led to days of "talking" via text. He made no attempt to meet me "offline," which led me to realize I was just filling in time for him. I was an escape from his boredom, and I cut it off.

Then there was the nice guy with whom I had decent conversations but very little else in common except for us both being college graduates. I could tell that he wasn't interested in anything serious, although he never voiced it. The conversation started to become shorter and more distant until things completely tapered off.

There was one particular guy who almost seemed sincere because he made me believe that he knew what he wanted.

I named him Mr. Sincere. He had a lot of questions and thoughts about my singleness. After getting me on a phone call, he interrogated me about

---

[1] Statista: https://www.statista.com/topics/2158/online-dating/

my decision to become abstinent in an attempt to change my mind. After realizing that I was not wavering in my vow with God to become abstinent, he asked me one more time, "Are you *really* not having sex until marriage?"

Before I could get the complete "Yes" out of my mouth, he hung up the phone like he was closing a Motorola flip phone. Although he wasn't a believer, his response to my choice to remain abstinent until marriage made me feel very insecure. I just knew that I wouldn't find a guy who was walking with the Lord or let alone valued my choice to be abstinent.

And then I met the guy who had everything going for himself: a great education, great looks, a great sense of style, humor, and a *relationship with God.* From the surface it appeared that I would be set for life with him, hence the name.

After having some deeper conversations about our Christian values, I determined that while he expressed a love for God, he also loved the things that God didn't. When it came to the topic of premarital sex and God's standard, he wasn't interested.

He didn't agree with the Bible's stance on celibacy, and this is a non-negotiable for me. I had to eventually cut ties with him. When I wasn't dating, I found it easier to believe that the man I envisioned spending my life with was out there somewhere. It wasn't until I tested the waters that I realized that the waters were troubled, Sis. I still didn't completely give up hope but my faith felt like it was running dry

Somewhere in my online dating journey, I heard God speak. He told me my future husband's name. I know, this felt as weird to me as it probably is to you as you read this. As I was praying for my future husband one day, God whispered his name to me. I thought I was hearing things the first time and He said it again. Now, although I hear God very clearly, I truly doubted I was hearing correctly. However, I decided I was going to trust His voice. Over time, I realized, in part, why God shared this information with me. It was to further weed out the men that would come along as I continued to date online and to encourage me to date with God

Up until this point, I had excluded God from my dating experience. What I mean by this is, that I wasn't seeking Him before further connecting with these men, in prayer. It may seem like a religious act to some but I realized the importance of presenting every relationship to him.

This can be as simple, as *God, help me to see what you desire me to do in this connection*. Or, *God, if this is for me please allow me to be opened to it if not please close this door*. There is no formula to dating with God, it's just important that you include Him in your journey. I believe God wants to give us wisdom with every decision we make. He wants to guide us to the best plans He has laid out for us. Why wouldn't we do this with dating?

Up until this point, I thought I had had my fair share of let-downs when it came to men, but clearly, I hadn't. One guy took getting to know me to a whole new level when he slid into my DMs. We chatted back and forth for a while and then escalated to him asking me out on a date. I was very intrigued by his forwardness. I love a good "make-plans" man instead of the incessant "wyd texts."

The first red flag of this entire connection was his words, "God highlighted you to me." I asked him what he meant by this because I was very confused, and he said, "you know, I don't look at too many women's pages like that, but God highlighted you to me." What this guy was saying was God told me to reach out to you. This is a very strong statement to make.

While I was very vulnerable at the time we connected, I made sure to get clarity from God this time with this connection. I needed to date with God on this one. I said, "God, if this is from you, please make it clear and if not, please give me wisdom." Things didn't end the same day I said the prayer; I had to keep seeking God.

After a few weeks of talking to this guy, I started to mention some communication issues we had. Ladies, this is not something I was used to. Instead of cutting him off and ghosting him, I had to admit to this guy how I felt about how he communicated to me.

I'd never been this vulnerable before, ever. I'd never said, how someone's actions made me feel in a relationship. I could point out what they did wrong but identifying how I felt and addressing it was very new for me.

This was the position that God was trying to get me to. He was developing a level of vulnerability in me that I desperately needed. When you date with God, you don't easily miss out on these lessons and opportunities for growth. This is the beauty in our singleness, regardless of how ugly it looks at times. We lean into the Lord and position ourselves to correct, heal, and develop.

So how did things eventually end with this guy and me? After a few conversations about our communication issues, he blurted out the truth. "I heard God wrong about you," he said. He also went on to admit that he'd been rejecting me.

This was the most heart-wrenching thing to hear, I felt completely blindsided and let down by him. But, while I was disappointed that another dating experience had ended, I learned a lot about myself in the process.

I learned what true vulnerability is from this experience. Advocating for yourself takes awareness, vulnerability, and confidence. It's not an easy thing to do, but it's so necessary. We are quick to say, "I'm okay," when we are not.

I learned to pause and assess how situations and people make me feel. Releasing my emotions and advocating for myself has been tough but so worth it. This may sound weird, but I finally feel like I'm moving past repressing emotions and allowing myself to feel, express myself, and then let it go.

REFLECTION

Dating God's way has not always been the easiest thing to do. I've dealt with my share of disappointments in myself, God, and the men I've dated. There've been countless times when I've walked away and questioned God. I've questioned God about His prospects for me. Whether there is someone out there for me who looks like Him. I've wanted to compromise so many times. I've wanted to give in to my fleshly desires so many times. I wanted to admit defeat with this abstinence journey countless times too, but by the grace of God I've held on.

God is not asking us to have this huge amount of faith in this area. God says that a mustard-sized amount of faith is enough to move mountains, that's all that's needed. I am grateful that God wrecks situations before He lets situations wreck us. He wants us to partner with Him if we choose to date so that we can gain what is needed in our seasons of singleness.

LET'S PRAY

Blessed Father, someone is reading this who feels like the disappointments they've faced in relationships are too great. They feel that they will never get your best, so they've decided to settle with what they see. Lord, I pray that you will encourage their heart. I believe that your desire is for them to seek you through every emotion they may be feeling at this moment. I pray that they will be encouraged into deeper intimacy with you. Give them an understanding of what your will is for them regarding marriage. Help them to embrace the unknown and partner with you in the present. You are a faithful, loving, and ever-present God, cause them to see this. Thank you for my sister reading this.

In Jesus' name, I pray, amen.

18.

Abstinent Men Do Exist

Society will tell you that you are crazy to wait on God for a spouse. They will tell you: "no man is going to be abstinent." They will tell you that it's better to "take what you can get." They will tell you: "the choices are slim." They will tell you: "your standards are too high." Society will laugh at the promises of God you stand on.

Don't be surprised when people doubt the vision that God has given you; He didn't give them your eyes. Having faith that God is going to bless you in your wait is going to take a lot of faith.

I've had people flat out tell me that what I desired in a man didn't exist. They've even gone as far as to say, "I don't think you know what you want."

What I've realized is that people give you advice based on their level of belief, vision, and experience. If you are talking to someone who dated and married without consulting with God, they may not understand your decision to seek God about your future mate. They may not be able to see things from your perspective or may just refuse to. If you are believing God for a man who is abstinent, God-fearing, honest, and has integrity, don't stop believing this because people don't validate your vision.

This reminds me of the story of Job in the bible. When Job lost everything: his home, his livestock, his good health, and his children, his friends had their own vision for Job's life. They swore, to Job, that his situation was a result of some sin in Job's life, even though the Word says that Job was blameless in the sight of the Lord. They were very pessimistic and attempted to sow seeds of doubt in Job's life. Their perspective was based on their perception and not God's divine will. Don't allow people to cast their fears onto you.

Regardless of what society or people say, Abstinent men do exist. You read that right, abstinent Christian men do exist, and they are not old, ugly, and undesirable. Abstinent men were a foreign idea, and for the longest time, I didn't think they existed until I went on a hunt to find them. I was pleasantly surprised to find Christian men who had made a vow to abstain from sex until they were married. I thought waiting for a man who valued God's word and abstained from sex (as a bare minimum) was an irrational thing to desire.

Culture, media, and the voices of others would only help me to hold tightly to the fallacy that there were no abstinent men in the world. Then God laid it on my heart to start an Instagram Live Series called *Celibate Men Do Exist*, and I deemed it an impossible mission. Where would I find men who were not old, not ugly, not undesirable, and abstinent?

A quick search on Google, YouTube, and Instagram led me to 3 amazing, God-fearing single, and abstinent men. My initial conversations with these men were one-on-one conversations via video conferencing and we talked about their walk with God, their decisions to become abstinent, their struggles, boundaries and so much more. The most surprising moment in these conversations, for me, was when I realized that men deal with the same issues women deal with.

Men need sex was the rhetoric I heard countless times in my long-term relationship. My ex-boyfriend often expressed that he didn't feel loved by me because I wasn't having sex with him.

There were moments in our relationship when he questioned my womanhood because I didn't desire to have sex with him. Sex equated to love to him and even before understanding the love of Christ, I couldn't buy into the fallacy that he made his reality. Before having these very open and honest conversations with these men, I was believing God for a man who shared my morals and values, a man I didn't have to force into a relationship with Christ, a man who valued my vow to abstain from sex until marriage, and a man who was unashamed about the gospel.

For these past few years, I truly leaped from doubt to faith that the man God had for me existed. Now, although none of the men who were a part of my IG live series was my husband, I was satisfied simply knowing that "God-grade" men do exist.

I once spoke to an abstinent man who stuck out most to me. He was refreshing. He told me he was raised by his stepfather. Although he had a male figure in his life, he expressed that there was so much more to gain from having his biological father around. He wondered if he'd missed out on life's lessons but also was secure that God was enough, and his life had panned out exactly how God intended it to.

This is what God's sovereignty looks like. Without having the voice of his biological father in his ear, he, like many inner-city men, looked to other men as the standard of what manhood is. Rap music painted a very misogynistic view of women which only helped to perpetuate this oversexualized identity that's often linked to manhood. This identity links one's manhood to whether or not they're having sex.

This was a common theme in conversations he would find amongst his friends and male influences. But this man knew he wanted to be different. He didn't want to live out what the world's standard of identity was.

God orchestrated his footsteps to get connected with a man of God who would help him reform his outlook on manhood by connecting his identity to Christ. He gave his life to God and started to notice an instant change in how he thought and felt. The things that his college teammates would participate in, he didn't find appealing. He was ready to truly be intentional about living his life for Christ. But what does this look like?

We hear the phrase, "living for Christ" thrown around often with "sacrificing your flesh," but what does this practically look like? He became intentional about giving up things that didn't align with what God said in His word, with pre-marital sex being one of them.

When I had my first conversation with him, I was under the assumption that he'd recently become abstinent because: Who besides me, had gone seven years without sex; let alone a man. I was under the assumption, again, that men only think about sex and cannot give up sex. I nearly fell out of my seat when he said he'd been abstinent for seven years also. You too have been abstinent for 7 years" I exclaimed; I thought I was the only person still standing. "God's grace" he responded. I knew exactly what he meant by this. God's grace is what empowers us to do what, in our minds, we feel is impossible to do.

Paul, who is my favorite person in the Bible aside from Jesus says to the Church at Corinth: *"My grace is sufficient for you, for my power is made perfect in weakness." Therefore I will boast all the more gladly about my weaknesses, so that Christ's power may rest on me.* (2 Corinthians 12:9)

Listen, Sis, you do not have to do abstinence alone when you have God and yes, you cannot abstain from sex; it is God's grace that gives you the ability to do so.

This man's testimony invalidates the expression that MEN cannot abstain from sex. His story shows us that we can do whatever we are intentional about. He did not express that he abstained from sex just to get married, even though that is his desire. He abstained from sex because he wanted to be intentional about his walk with God. Although I haven't met my person yet, I believe that he's out there. I believe that, and he is a man who is chasing after God's heart. I believe that he is a man who values his relationship with God and takes his walk seriously. I want the same for you.

REFLECTION

On your journey of singleness, you may experience opposition to your faith. The world is going to speak things to you that may be very contrary to what you are believing God for. Even with the seeds of doubt that people may sow into your life, you must stand on God's truth. God's truth concerning your future marriage is the thing that He's promised you. Even when it doesn't appear as if things are working out in your favor regarding your future marriage, you still should trust God. You should trust God even if those closest to you are not believing God's best for you, just like Job. You read the account of one gentleman from my Instagram Live series wo

LET'S PRAY

Heavenly Father, I pray for my sister who is reading this right now. She may have allowed the lies of the enemy or the opposition from others to cause her to stop believing. I pray, that she will be reminded of the promises you've made to her. I pray that she will not grow weary in doing right. Empower her with the capacity to wait on you. Give her the grace to be still and know that you are God. I pray that she will surrender her love story to you and trust you with it. May she no longer try to control the narrative but surrender it all at your feet, dear God.

You are good and your compassion toward us never fails. You see your daughter's heart. You know where disappointment has set in. I pray that you will alleviate the burdens she's been carrying.

Eyes have not seen, ears have not heard and neither has it entered in her heart that which you have for her. Help her to have faith in the unheard, unseen, and unfathomable.

In Jesus' name, I pray. Amen.

19.

Ready, Set, Wait

One of the biggest revelations I have had during my abstinence journey is that I need God. You cannot do this by your own strength. I thought I could do it on my own. Oh, was I wrong! I thought I was good until reality hit me and I had to pray to God to give me the strength to keep my vow. I continually acknowledge that I need God. When we do this, it gives God the permission to step in and help us, He's not going to force himself on us. Has the journey been easy?

Absolutely not, but I'm in it with Him this time. When I pray, I don't ask God to remove the desire I ask Him to help me not to act on it. What you're feeling is normal. Listen, Paul said: "I do not understand what I do. For what I want to do I do not do, but what I hate I do" in Romans 5:17.

God knows the "struggle is real?" He says, 'No temptation has overtaken you but that which is common to man but for every temptation, I give you a way of escape." Remember Mr. Hot Chocolate? My way out of going up for a nightcap with him was to call a cab to take me home.

What is it that God has promised you during a time of doubt or disbelief? Did God place a desire in your heart for a business? Did God plant the seed of a goal in your mind? Did God place love in your heart for ministry? Just because you're waiting for a spouse, it doesn't mean that everything needs to be placed on hold. Even when things appear to be contrary to what God promised, this doesn't mean that God's promise is impossible. God's promise is just that, a PROMISE.

> "For no matter how many promises God has made, they are "Yes" in Christ. And so through Him the "Amen" is spoken by us to the glory of God." (2 Corinthians 1:20 NIV)

In Genesis chapter 18, the Lord said this to Abraham regarding his wife Sarah, "Why did Sarah laugh and say, 'Will I really have a child, now that I am old?' Is anything too hard for the Lord? I will return to you at the appointed time next year, and Sarah will have a son." Sarah was afraid, so she lied and said, "I did not laugh." But he said, "Yes, you did laugh." Sarah doubted what God said because she couldn't see past the circumstance of her old age. God's response, to

Sarah, was: "Is there anything too hard for me?" God was asking Sarah what He already knew to determine her level of faith in Him. Sometimes God will test your belief in His promise to you.

If you are anything like me, you've felt like you've been in the waiting room of life just hoping that your name is called. You may even feel like life is passing you by and everyone is advancing but you. These are all the things the enemy feeds us in an attempt to make us anxious, fearful, and move out of God's will. In dating, this would be us settling for less than God's best.

There were many points in my singleness when I became extremely frustrated while waiting on God. Sarah's laugh was my cry to God many times. I've often heard women say: "If God never brings me someone, I will be fine with just Him," that was never my testimony.

As much as I love God, I also had this strong desire to be married. So I called out to God, and I laid my desires at His feet, I cried "God, this desire to be married is completely overtaking me, if this is not something you want for me; please remove this desire." The desire never left; this was a sign to me that I needed to continue to wait.

There is nothing too hard for God. Don't let delay cause you to doubt the promises of God. If you know God said it, don't doubt Him for it. In between the promise and the birth of their son Isaac, Abraham prayed for the sinful city Sodom and Gomorrah. In between leaving her hometown and meeting her husband Boaz, Ruth found herself working in the field.

I wish I could throw away every notion that says, "you must be perfect before God will send you a husband," or the phrase, "you need to get yourself together" or "be content in your singleness so you can be content in your marriage." My key encouragement to you would rather be a question: what are you going to do while you wait? During Abraham's waiting season, he didn't wallow in doubt. Abraham was active in the work of the Lord, as was Ruth. This shows us a great example of what we should do while we "wait."

If you continue to read the story of Abraham and Sarah, you will discover that they decided to take matters into their own hands. Instead of waiting on God's promise, insecure Sarah begged her husband to sleep with her handmaid and bear a child. Hagar birthed Abraham's son Ishmael, who stands today as a symbol of what happens when you don't wait on God.

Don't birth an Ishmael while you wait, wait in faith on the promise, Isaac. "Sarah became pregnant and bore a son to Abraham in his old age, **at the very time God had promised him.**" (Genesis 21:2.) God does not break his promises. As it was with Sarah and Abraham, so it will be with you. Between the word/promise and the manifested promise was time. Sarah and Abraham had to wait until God's appointed time. **Waiting is inevitable but what will you do while you wait?**

Reading the letters from Paul helped me put my singleness in perspective from a biblical lens. Paul goes into further detail about the instructions on marriage in his letter to the church at Corinth:

> I want you to be free from the concerns of this life. An unmarried man can spend his time doing the Lord's work and thinking how to please him. But a married man has to think about his earthly responsibilities and how to please his wife. His interests are divided. In the same way, a woman who is no longer married or has never been married can be devoted to the Lord and holy in body and in spirit. But a married woman has to think about her earthly responsibilities and how to please her husband. I am saying this for your benefit, not to place restrictions on you. I want you to do whatever will help you serve the Lord best, with as few distractions as possible. (1 Corinthians 7:32-35 NLT)

Paul mentions three things that we *can* do while we are single: be devoted to the Lord, be holy in body, and be holy in spirit. Being devoted to the Lord does not always feel like this heavy burden weighing you down. It isn't attending church every Sunday, reading your Bible for 10 hours every day, and praying for 6. While all of those things are great, God is more concerned about your heart condition. Do you desire to devote your life to the Lord? Often people resist accepting Christ because they fear what they will lose in the process. They look at what they will lose instead of all that they will gain.

God wants your heart to be devoted primarily to Him. God wants to know that He has all of you. He wants you to prioritize your time with Him, He wants to feel as if you desire to put Him first. Your organic heart devotion to God will be exemplified in your actions but not the other way around.

This is important to know because a lot of us single people feel as if we need to do more in order to get. We often feel like we are single because we don't spend enough time with God, we aren't healed, we need to work on ourselves, etc. The truth may be as simple as, it's just not the time. While you wait, do as Paul did – devote yourself to The Lord. Your devotion to God will bring about supernatural change in your life. As you go deeper in intimacy with God you will begin to see transformation in your life – I can attest to this.

In my singleness, I've realized that I had two choices: I could date as the world dates, or I could wait on God's best. I could wait for my Isaac, or I could settle for my Ishmael. For many years, I dated from the lens of abandonment and rejection which led to much heartache and disappointment. It was during my time of waiting and enduring, that I learned the most about myself; my greatest healing was **done** in my seasons of patient waiting.

The time between the problem and the promise is your training ground; it's a spiritual obstacle course complete with intervals of situations and opportunities that mold us into who God wants us to be. Many of us are "in-training" right now; we are being prepared to be wives; God is doing the work on our hearts and in our minds.

Equally Yoked

In my season of waiting, I don't have a type anymore. When asked, as often as I'm asked, "what is your type?" I say, Christ. Christ is my type. I've been seeing everything but Christ in these men I've been encountering. "Your standards are too high," they say. If integrity, respect, leadership, and a heart for God are too much to ask for then I'd much rather stay single than settle.

I cannot stress the following statement enough: "know who you are and whose you are." It is so important when dating (or just in general), that you have a clear understanding of your worth. Ladies, it's time for us to know who we are and what we deserve. After acknowledging your worth, you must then put your self-confidence into action. A man who has no good intentions will try to plant seeds of doubt, about your wait or standards, in you. My many encounters with men and stories from my girlfriends solidify the weight of that last statement.

No matter how long you've been single, don't ever get to the place where you are desperate. With desperation comes a vulnerability to lower the standards of what you deserve.

I went on a date with this guy once; whom I later found out intentions weren't pure! In conversation, he asked the infamous and dreaded question: "So, why are you still single?"

My response was, as it usually is: "I'm waiting to encounter a man who meets the basic standards of what I'm looking for."

"So, what is it that you are looking for?" he asked.

"The basics: honesty, integrity, ambition, and morals," I responded.

He didn't seem too enthused by my response.

A man who can't or is unwilling to meet the standards you set will try to make you feel you're asking for too much. You are not asking for too much, girl. A man should be willing to bring to the table the same things you are offering. The basics are expected: honesty, integrity, morals, and values. Don't allow a man to make you feel like he can hand you the short end of the stick and never feel obliged to accept it. I'm too old for Netflix and chill boy---make plans. I came to remind you of who you are! The days of accepting scraps are over.

Once on a date, I didn't intend on bringing my choice to be abstinent up but after some probing, it surfaced. His response to me expressing I was abstinent was: "Oh, men like that don't exist anymore" but what I heard was: "You might as well just give it up to me because there's no hope for you." He then proceeded to disgust me even further with his next statement: "Marriage is just a piece of paper."

"Well, if you believe that's the case, then I'd rather stay single than give it up to a guy who doesn't meet my standards," I responded.

Without getting into details, like finding out halfway through the dinner that he was still legally married, he didn't meet my standards, and the date was cut short.

Here are some more lies I've heard from men:

You're never going to find a man like that

Your standards are too high

You are expecting too much

Yeah, no one believes in THAT anymore

Those types of men don't exist

Wait on a man that will love you the way that God loves you. God is concerned with every single aspect of who you are. He's fully concerned about your mental, physical, and spiritual well-being. Fall in love with God first, not the idea of love. If you want a "God" relationship, get to know God. A man should treat you the way that God values you. You're not just worth it, you're MORE than worth it. Not sure of how you should be treated, spend time with God.

So maybe you're reading this and you're struggling with low self-esteem, I've been there before. It was when I began to spend time with God that He shed the layers of self-doubt and low self-worth off of me. Stop comparing yourself to the girls you see on social media. Stop decreasing your worth because he left you. Your worth is not based on the men you are/aren't in a relationship with, your worth comes from God. You alone are precious in the sight of God.

Someday you will see yourself the way that God sees you. How about you let that someday be today.

Love yourself for the woman you are and stop waiting on someone to love you back in return. The person God DOES have for you, you'll never have to compromise yourself or shrink back to be with. They will see the value and beauty in you. Best of all, they will recognize the God in you.

Until then, remember this: you don't need anything or anyone to validate you. You don't have to worry about gaining anyone's love. Your purpose is waiting for you. It's waiting for you to stop focusing on your loneliness, what you're lacking, and what you think everyone else has and focus on you. Your day will come beloved. God has heard your prayers. Not one of your tears has gone unnoticed. He's seen them all. Not only that but he's seen who's left you out to dry, He's seen who has disregarded you, He's seen who's mistreated you and He wants you to LET IT GO and Let HIM avenge you. Men with integrity do exist. Honest men do exist and men who are willing to wait: DO EXIST.

REFLECTION

Just because you're waiting for a spouse doesn't mean that everything needs to be placed on hold. I've witnessed so many amazing and beautiful women whose lives were on hold because they were waiting for a man. "Oh, I won't buy a home until I'm married," "I won't start this business until my husband comes," "I'm waiting until I'm married to travel there," and the list goes on.

I'm not speaking from a mountain here; I was this woman too. I wanted to put my life on hold until I got married. But what are you going to do while you wait? Are you going to remain idle until marriage or are you going to get out and explore the world?

Don't put your life on hold, Sis.

Do all the things you want to do NOW. Travel, try new cuisines, write that book, start that fashion line, and start that business. I am believing that the man that God has for you will appreciate how multidimensional you are.

You are not doing these things to be in the "I can do better on my own" camp but rather because you deserve it. You deserve to go places you've never been before and to meet people you've never met. People are waiting on you to step into your God-ordained calling. You've been sitting, stalling, waiting, and worrying.

Please let this be a defining moment for you, where you quit just waiting and start living while you wait.

LET'S PRAY

Dear God, thank you for being so intentional when it comes to me. In your Word, you say "when I consider thy heavens, the work of thy fingers, the moon, and the stars, which thou hast ordained; What is man, that thou art mindful of him? You've created this whole world, yet you care about me. Thank you, Lord. I pray that you will align resources that will allow me to explore this beautiful world that you've created. I pray that I will have the faith to sit aimlessly in despair waiting for a husband, no longer.

I pray that I will trust you completely with my love story. From this moment forward, I will no longer put the purpose for which you created me on hold. Wherever you call me, I will go. I surrender my singleness to you, God. May you get the glory out of this season just as you will with my future marriage. In Jesus' name, I pray, Amen.

20.

Preparing Your Heart for Marriage

If you want the God thing, then know that the God "thing" takes time. I do not believe in the rhetoric that tells women to fix themselves and he will come. However, I do believe that our singleness is a time to heal, stretch, and grow. So, we shouldn't run into relationships without allowing God to prepare and process us. This is because God wants us to be fully equipped for the marriage ministry.

And yes, marriage is a ministry. It is a position that comes with many different responsibilities. This dates back to the creation story in Genesis when God gave Adam a role in the garden and then brought him a helpmate to accomplish the task. You and your spouse are joined together to serve and bring glory and honor to God. God instructs that a man must love His wife like God loves the church; that's ministry.

Marriage is selfless. Are you ready to give your complete self to another individual? I had to ask myself this question too! Am I ready to give up the ability to make decisions solely on my own without having to consider a partner? If you're praying for a "Godly" relationship, are you ready to "submit yourselves to your own husbands so that, if any of them do not believe the word, they may be won over without words but by the behavior of their wives? (1 Peter 3:1)

A friend once said that she had to cross over from doubt to faith on her journey to being married. She desired marriage and believed that God would give her the desires of her heart. Her desire for marriage was in line with the desire God had placed in her heart, or at least that's what I assumed. Even as I write the pages of this book, I can have moments where I *still* struggle with doubting that God has someone for me. Hebrews 11 says: faith is the substance of things hoped for and the evidence of things not seen. So, to have faith in God is the sum of the things that you don't see but still believe him for.

Although I believe God is a sovereign God whose ways are perfect for me, this did not stop me from having fears and doubts that I would ever get married. I had to constantly and consciously make the choice to trust God in the area of my singleness. Whenever doubt crept in, I had to learn to let go of how I expected my love life to look. I had to intentionally believe that God would manifest everything he has promised.

I truly believe that it is God's will, and I make a conscious effort to march toward that belief. How can I be sure that there was a change in me? Well, over time,

I've noticed that my response to situations has changed. I no longer feel this overwhelming anxiety regarding my future marriage.

I don't feel desperate about my future marriage. I understand that if it is God's will for me to be single for the rest of my life, then God would give me the grace to be single for the rest of my life. But because I'm trusting that his will is for me to wed, I am okay in my moments of weakness. Every time I feel doubt or weakness, I'm reminded that this position is just temporary and that it won't always be like this.

No amount of books, sermons, or YouTube series will cause you to believe in God for your future marriage. It must be something you desire. And if it is something you desire, then you must make a personal decision today to trust God for it. And guess what? If your faith runs out tomorrow, that's okay too. God has enough faith and strength for you. Paul says it best in 2 Corinthians:

> "Three different times I begged the Lord to take it away. Each time he said, "My grace is all you need. My power works best in weakness." So now I am glad to boast about my weaknesses, so that the power of Christ can work through me. That's why I take pleasure in my

weaknesses, and in the insults,
hardships, persecutions, and troubles
that I suffer for Christ. For when I am
weak, then I am strong." (2 Corinthians
12:8-10 NLT)

Every time we are weak, it's an indication that
we don't have it all. It's a cue for us to seek God!

I cannot say that I know or comprehend
everything that God does, but I do know that God
doesn't work according to human logic. He doesn't do
the easy things or the realistic things, He operates off of
what seems impossible. I truly believe that God will
make it seem impossible, and make others think it will
never happen, just to show that He is God. God steps in
when it seems like all hope is lost, not to stress us out
or frustrate us but to prove to us, and everyone around
us, that He is God.

One of the practices I put into place during my
singleness was fasting. I fasted for myself, my marriage,
and my future husband. Fasting is a way to put our
flesh under subjection. Fasting is a way to deny what
our flesh wants to do (our desire to have sex for
example) and empowers our spirit.

When you are operating in the spirit, you can
tap into God's perfect will for your life. The spirit that is

working in and through you will lead you on a path to wholeness, complete healing, and Godly success.

Fasting is a strategy of spiritual warfare, it helps us to fight against the enemy. For example, if there are generational curses in your family, cycles of abuse, abandonment, and divorces; fasting can break it from happening to you.

When you fast, you are taking your authority in Christ, you are showing the enemy who you are and you are taking back what belongs to you. Fasting can give you clarity, revelation, strength, endurance, and breakthrough.

With that, I would like to encourage you, if you haven't, to devote some time to fasting. This fast that you will find below was designed to allow you the space and time for reflection. Too often we ask people for advice when what we need is found in God. As you read through this book I want you to take your time to think, ask God questions, write, and reflect; this will ensure that you truly receive what God has for you and not my words alone

So, why do we fast? We are both flesh and spirit in one body. Our flesh is a combination of our desires which are contrary to God's will for us. Our flesh is selfish, it does what it wants to satisfy itself. Our spirit is aligned with God and makes decisions according to Godly wisdom. Our spirit has to be constantly fed to operate. We want to ensure that our spirit is always active and aware so that our actions lead us on the path that God has for us.

Matthew 17:21 21 (KJV) says, *"How be it this kind goeth not out but by prayer and fasting."* Some things will not change until we fast and pray about them. Fasting is a spiritual principle that builds muscle in us and suppresses our flesh so that we can hear God speaking clearly.

There are many different ways that you can fast. These are the strategies I implement when fasting.

Fast Details:

- Abstain from food (6 am – 6 pm) or (12 am – 12 pm) or sun up to sundown.
- Include morning and evening prayers with prayer points. Including the prayer points that will help to make your prayer more directional. For instance, when I pray for my future husband, I pray for his mind, hands, heart, ministry, career, and relationship with God. I intentionally focus on these areas in prayer.

Prophetic journaling is another strategy for fasting where you write what you hear God saying. I open my journal and I start with my prayer + words to God and then I write what I believe I hear God saying.

Personal reflection + introspection are key when fasting and praying. We often feel many different emotions tied to our past relationships and are triggered by certain things. When triggered, I like to sit and explore what I am feeling and what I believe triggered that emotion. This practice has helped me to get to the root cause of my emotions, why am I feeling what I am feeling, and how can God heal me in this area.

Sis, it's time to take control of your love life and to start praying for your marriage. No longer will you allow your marital status to hold you captive or fill you with shame. No longer will you question your worth because you have not yet been found. No longer will you doubt that God hears you because you see so many others obtaining what you desire to obtain. Today is the day to surrender your love story and your desire for marriage over to God.

If you decide to fast, take some time to implement the above strategy or pray to God for direction for one of your own. Over the next seven days, start to explore the topics in this book that have tugged at your heart. What things have triggered you? What things hit home for you? Explore these topics in your journal and prayer time with God. Take the next seven (7) days to fast, seek intimacy with God, and pray strategically for your husband.

Purposeful Prayer:

Lord God, I thank you for your sovereignty. I know that nothing you do is by accident or coincidence; everything is for a purpose. Lord, help me to embrace the purpose of my life and the purpose of my singleness. Help me to focus less on what others have and what others are doing and focus more on me. Help me to embrace every aspect of my singleness. Help me to use my time alone to my benefit.

Now, God, prepare me to be the woman you have created me to be. Mend everything in me that is broken so that I no longer look to things to fill any void. Let this fast be a turning point in my history. Let this be the moment where everything shifts for me.

Bring fresh revelation, clarity, understanding, and vision with this fast. I pray that if your desire for me is marriage, you will help prepare me to be the wife you have destined me to be and you will reveal this to me after this fast I pray this prayer in Jesus' name. Amen.

Here is the prayer I prayed for my future husband:

God, I thank you for my God-ordained husband. God, I thank you for protecting him. I thank you for covering him. I thank you for giving him a mind of wisdom and a mind of knowledge. I pray that you will bless his hands in all that he does. I pray that everything He touches will be a success. I pray that you will bless his eyes so that he will keep his attention and focus solely on you and the purpose you've given him. God, I pray that you will bless and protect his heart so that it will not be contaminated by the ways of this world. I pray that you will bless his feet so that wherever he goes, he is stepping into a realm of success and opportunity.

I pray that you will make him a man of integrity, a man of honor, and a man of humility. I bind the spirit of pride and ego from his life O God. God, give him the desires of his heart. Keep him on the straight and narrow path. God, expand his mind and fill it with divine ideas, visions, and dreams. Mold him into a man that has a heart for you and your people, God. Anoint and empower him for ministry. Give him a thirst for your word. I pray that you will mold and shape him into a leader, equip him to be a priest over his home, and empower him to be an influence in his community. I thank you in advance for keeping him for me and me for him. In Jesus' name. Amen.

Here's what I want for you, Sis: I want you to be the woman of God that He intends for you to be! I want your desire for marriage to be fulfilled. I want you to grow in Christ while you are waiting. I want you to have confidence in your purpose so much that the doubts of others do not shake your faith. Yes, singleness gets lonely sometimes, but I don't want you to spend your time sulking in singleness when you can be exploring your purpose. You're living for a purpose and if you do not take the time to discover that purpose then your living will be in vain. After all, there is so much that goes into being a wife that we must consider before we jump into a marriage.

I'm ministering to you the same way I've ministered to myself countless times. I'm human and, sometimes, being single gets lonely, but I've learned to embrace my singleness. I have moments of weakness, but when I think about my marriage, I want God to be completely in it; I don't want any man who is not sent from Him.

Marriage is the goal, but what will you do while you wait?

21.

Let God Write Your Love Story

If God gives you a desire for marriage, then He will bring you a spouse. It is that simple.

I remember the day I prayed and asked God to take away my desire to get married. I cried out: "God, if you are not going to bring me a spouse, if this is not your will for me, remove the desire and I will be okay."

He didn't.

The word of God says that He will give you the desires of your heart. When God gives you the desires of your heart, he is downloading His desire for you into your heart. He places that desire there; desires that line up with the will of God.

Many Christians have argued this point saying they don't want to give false hope. My job is to encourage you to believe God will bring you a spouse. God's desire is for us to replenish the Earth through His ordained marriages. I stand on the word of God and so should you.

As cliché as it may sound: God's timing is perfect. Throughout the word of God, we find many situations where God exemplifies his sovereignty. My favorite scripture that points to God's sovereignty is Job 38 (NLT). Job was a faithful man of God who lost everything in a moment: his children, his animals, his success, his wealth, and his health.

In 37 chapters of the Book of Job, Job is complaining to both God and his friends about his unfortunate chain of events. While Job is complaining to God, God remains silent until chapter 38 when He speaks:

The Lord Challenges Job

38 Then the Lord answered Job from the whirlwind:

2 "Who is this that questions my wisdom

with such ignorant words?

3 Brace yourself like a man,

because I have some questions for you,

and you must answer them.

4 "Where were you when I laid the foundations of the earth?

Tell me, if you know so much.

5 Who determined its dimensions

and stretched out the surveying line?

6 What supports its foundations,

and who laid its cornerstone

7 as the morning stars sang together

and all the angels[a] shouted for joy?

8 "Who kept the sea inside its boundaries

as it burst from the womb,

9 and as I clothed it with clouds

and wrapped it in thick darkness?

10 For I locked it behind barred gates,

limiting its shores.

11 I said, 'This far and no farther will you come.

Here your proud waves must stop!'

12 "Have you ever commanded the morning to appear

and caused the dawn to rise in the east?

13 Have you made daylight spread to the ends of the earth,

to bring an end to the night's wickedness?

14 As the light approaches,

the earth takes shape like clay pressed beneath a seal;

it is robed in brilliant colors.[b]

15 The light disturbs the wicked

and stops the arm that is raised in violence.

16 "Have you explored the springs from which the seas come?

Have you explored their depths?

17 Do you know where the gates of death are located?

Have you seen the gates of utter gloom?

18 Do you realize the extent of the earth?

Tell me about it if you know!

19 "Where does light come from,

and where does darkness go?

20 Can you take each to its home?

Do you know how to get there?

21 But of course you know all this!

For you were born before it was all created,

and you are so very experienced!

22 "Have you visited the storehouses of the snow

or seen the storehouses of hail?

23 (I have reserved them as weapons for the time of trouble,

for the day of battle and war.)

²⁴ Where is the path to the source of light?

Where is the home of the east wind?

²⁵ "Who created a channel for the torrents of
rain?

Who laid out the path for the lightning?

²⁶ Who makes the rain fall on barren land,

in a desert where no one lives?

²⁷ Who sends rain to satisfy the parched ground

and make the tender grass spring up?

²⁸ "Does the rain have a father?

Who gives birth to the dew?

²⁹ Who is the mother of the ice?

Who gives birth to the frost from the heavens?

³⁰ For the water turns to ice as hard as rock,

and the surface of the water freezes.

³¹ "Can you direct the movement of the stars—

binding the cluster of the Pleiades

or loosening the cords of Orion?

³² Can you direct the constellations through the
seasons

or guide the Bear with her cubs across the heavens?

³³ Do you know the laws of the universe?

Can you use them to regulate the earth?

³⁴ "Can you shout to the clouds

and make it rain?

³⁵ Can you make lightning appear

and cause it to strike as you direct?

³⁶ Who gives intuition to the heart

and instinct to the mind?

³⁷ Who is wise enough to count all the clouds?

Who can tilt the water jars of heaven?

³⁸ when the parched ground is dry

and the soil has hardened into clods?

³⁹ "Can you stalk prey for a lioness

and satisfy the young lions' appetites

⁴⁰ as they lie in their dens

or crouch in the thicket?

⁴¹ Who provides food for the ravens

when their young cry out to God

and wander about in hunger?

If God is in control of the land and the sea, the birds in the sky, the rain; sun, moon, and snow, does He not have our love lives under control? His perfect control.

Omniscience is the divine distinction between God and man. God sees the beginning from the end and the end from the beginning. Revelation 22:13 ESV says I am the Alpha and the Omega, the first and the last, the beginning and the end." He knows our future and desires to guide us into His perfect will for it. The future that God sees for you does not omit your love life.

Sometimes we may feel like God has everything under control but our love life. If you are anything like me, you trust God in every other area of your life aside from your love life. Why is this? Could it be because we've experienced constant disappointments?

I'd say that this has something to do with our lack of faith in this area. Letting God write your love story consists of you surrendering your timeline and will to God, waiting on him to bring his promises alive, and not taking matters into your own hands.

Surrendering to God's Will and Time

I believe that everything in life starts to happen when it's supposed to! Surrendering your will over to God is a conscious decision to follow God's voice and His plan regardless of how it looks. Do you know why we get frustrated about life so much? It is because we have too many expectations about how things are supposed to work out -- I am guilty of this!

When you allow your expectations to supersede God's plans, you place God in a box. One of my favorite scriptures is Ephesians 3:20 (NIV), "Now to him who is able to do immeasurably more than all we ask or imagine, according to his power that is at work within us." This alone should encourage you to stop thinking too much. What God can do will always pale in comparison to what our finite minds can conjure up.

So, "Trust in the Lord with all your heart and lean not on your own understanding; In all your ways submit to him, and he will make your paths straight." (Proverbs 3:4-6 - NLT)

When I quit my career as a social worker, I thought I was supposed to find another job in the field (finite mind). After months of hearing 'no' at every turn, I decided to give up and be still (surrender). I didn't know that I was surrendering; I only knew that I'd given up trying to work things out in my own strength. In my stillness, God spoke to me.

"Start a blog," He said.

I fought through a lot of self-doubt and disappointment as I put my fingers to the keyboard to type.

I asked, "What will they think about my writing?"

I asked. "Who will read it?"

And I told myself: "I'm scared."

I didn't know that a small act of faith would produce the results that I am seeing today. This same faith is needed in your singleness. The faith to set aside your marital plans and do what God is telling you to do today. Pick up the pen, get the notepad and start writing today; not your goals, but seek God's will for your life while you are single.

So many things in my life hadn't worked out as planned and I felt the blog would be added to that list. Instead of surrendering to the negative thoughts, I surrendered my will to God. This act alone opened doors for me beyond my wildest dreams (*exceedingly abundantly*). I had no idea what I was doing when I started the blog, I only knew I needed to follow that inner voice (God's will). I challenge you to surrender your desire for marriage over to God. Ask God to take the wheel in your season of singleness. Pray that He gives you divine strategies on how to navigate it and the grace to *wait in joy*. It is through your full surrender that God can do His best work in your life. God cannot touch it if you still have your hands on it; make room for God and surrender.

Years ago, God gave me a vision for my marriage. When it didn't happen in years one, two, three, four, and five, I was okay but when year six crept up, my endurance started to run out. God reminded me to write down the vision and remember the promise.

If I could pull a page out of my journal it would've read, "God, what do I do when what I see does not line up with the vision you've given me? How is it humanly possible that you will bring me a spouse when all I've encountered are counterfeits, men pretending to be something they're not?" "How is it humanly possible that you will bring me a spouse when I've dealt with nothing but constant let-downs and disappointments. Why not me?"

Everyone's getting married…but me.

Everyone is in relationships…but me.

Everyone is having children…but me.

Everyone is getting ahead…but me.

Everyone is getting blessed…but me.

We have all been, at some point, guilty of coveting or desiring what someone else has based on what we see on social media. We subconsciously live our lives vicariously through people we don't know.

Comparison becomes deadly when we start to believe that we are behind life's schedule. Behind Instagram filters and social media highlight "reels" are real-life situations. We don't always know what's happening in the relationships we are hash-tagging #relationshipgoals. Everyone isn't always posting about the struggles, the arguments, the battles, the sleepless nights, and the prayers for their husbands to come home. **What we see is a curated version of their best captured moments.**

The enemy wants you to compare what you have with what someone else has! He does this because if you are focused on what another individual has you will never seek or find the fullness of what God has for you! Rubbernecking takes your eyes off the road— think about it.

If you've made up your mind to chase after God, you are where you need to be at this very moment. You are not missing any blessings and you certainly aren't lacking anything. You are not in competition with anyone for the blessings that God has for you! Let the success of others be an inspiration to you of what God can do. Kill comparison before it kills your dreams!

Here are 7 things I wish I would have spent more time doing earlier on in my singleness:

1. Not being fixated on marriage so much
2. Not involving myself with men that weren't worthy of my time and energy.
3. Being focused on my career.
4. Spent more time with God while allowing him to uncover my purpose and free me from soul ties, unforgiveness, resentment, idolatry, childhood trauma, and abandonment.
5. Invested in living and leave the writing of the love story to God.
6. Stopped settling for second best
7. Stopped minimizing who I was just so I could be accepted by men.

We must have hope and trust that God has someone for us, wherever He may be hiding. The Bible says: It is not good for man to be alone. That is a promise from God, and so we need to remind God of His promise. God, your word says: It's not good for me to be alone. Make me a helpmate Lord. Develop your relationship with God. Find out what gift God has given you. Start to invest in your dream. I think the worst thing we can do is stop living until someone comes and sweeps us off of our feet.

Don't worry about what was lost

"God, your God, will restore everything you lost; he'll have compassion on you; he'll come back and pick up the pieces from all the places where you were scattered." (Deuteronomy 30:3 MSG)

I've spent years sacrificing, dedicating my life to God, disciplining myself; selflessly giving my time, energy, and ear with no immediate reward. I've watched others get blessed and cried out to God "What about me?" I've gotten weary and tired of doing the right things all the time. There were times when I just wanted to give up doing things God's way – throw His whole plan away. There were times when I doubted that God heard my prayers and was going to be faithful enough to answer them.

For years, I had to blindly follow God even though it didn't make sense; things weren't fully adding up, but I rested on God's promises. I certainly have not arrived, but I am exactly where God promised me that I would be. His blessings are overtaking me and because I've waited for it, I have received the fullness of it. The things I've lost look small in comparison to what I've gained. Small, Sis!

I don't even desire to have what God took from me because He has blessed me with so much more! I want to encourage you to hold on, stop looking at what everyone else has, and trust God's plan for your life. Don't give up yet.

Don't Awaken Love Before the Right Time

Young women of Jerusalem, I charge you, do not stir up or awaken love until the appropriate time. Song of Solomon 8:4 (CSB). **Awakening love before its time seems like our natural tendency**, if our hands are not in it, we feel it will not get done. How is God going to work this out? How will He bring me a spouse if I am not doing the work?

I wish I'd heeded Solomon's warning earlier on in my single season. This would have helped me to avoid a lot of heartbreak and disappointment. Sometimes we can feel as if God is trying to withhold some good thing from us when in fact, He withholds no good thing. We don't realize that closed doors are just as good as opened doors.

There are ways that God protects us through "missed opportunities" that we may never understand. There were some relationships, you were in, that had to end to protect you. I thank God for ending some of the situationships that I didn't have the strength to end on my own.

Through my experience, I understand why God instructs us, women, not to awaken love before its time. This scripture is God telling us: don't struggle to open a door that is not meant for you to open. You don't have to beg, con, or bribe a man to love you or see you. I know that culture will ask you: How will you ever find love if you stay home all the time?" and "If you want to find a man, you need to get out more." The "get out more" comment is what led me on a wild goose chase trying to find love.

I was so desperate to awaken love before its time that I found myself "sliding in the DM's" of countless men. I lied to myself by thinking it was harmless flirting. All the time I spent trying to awaken love, not only wasted my time but it left me disappointed and running to God with a broken heart.

There were so many times, on this journey, that the enemy sent distractions on my path to derail me from God's best and they were wrapped up in the "perfect" package. Do what works best for you with the help of God.

As for me, I know that I cannot "put myself out there" or "shoot my shot," I prefer to wait on God's best no matter how crazy I may look to others. God knows what's best for us even when it doesn't feel like it. Surrender your love story to God, I know how hard it is to be single and alone. I know the painful feeling of loneliness; you are not alone.

One question remains though, when *is* the right time? As we peruse the pages of the Bible, we often find many stories that indicate the importance of time as it relates to God.

King Solomon who is thought to be one of the wisest men of the Bible wrote Ecclesiastes. This book sheds light on some very humanistic questions we've most likely pondered or asked ourselves. In 12 short chapters, Solomon challenges how we think about the world and our motives. He watched the sun rise and set for years and took notice of human motives and behaviors. In chapter 3 of the book, Solomon writes,

"For everything there is a season, and a time for every [a]purpose under heaven: 2 a time to be born, and a time to die; a time to plant, and a time to pluck up that which is planted; 3 a time to kill, and a time to heal; a time to break down, and a time to build up; 4 a time to weep, and a time to laugh; a time to mourn, and a time to dance; 5 a time to cast away stones, and a time to gather stones together; a time to embrace, and a time to refrain from embracing; 6 a time to seek, and a time to lose; a time to keep, and a time to cast away; 7 a time to rend, and a time to sew; a time to keep silence, and a time to speak; 8 a time to love, and a time to hate; a time for war, and a time for peace." (Ecclesiastes 3:1-8 ESV)

What is he saying to us here and how can this be applied to our singleness journey? We shouldn't rush into relationships or marriage outside of God's time. God wants you to be fully equipped for ministry. Yes, "marriage" is a ministry first. You and your spouse are joined to serve together. You and your spouse are joined together to bring glory and honor to God. God instructs that a man must love His wife like God loves the church; that's ministry. Marriage is selfless.

Are you ready to give your complete self to another individual? Are you ready to compromise? Are you ready to communicate openly and confront hard situations? **Are you ready to submit to the leadership of your husband who is under the leadership of God?** The wait is what prepares you for this. He's working on you and your spouse's heart. He's healing you and your spouse's trauma.

When God deems it time to bring a matter into existence, He will. Until then, we are to enjoy the season we are in. Perhaps you are in your "time to plant season." In my time to plant season, I laid down the seeds for this; I began sharing my story on my various social media platforms and offline at various events. Sharing my story and expressing the hope for future marriage were the seeds that I planted in my "planting" season. I began to lay the foundation for this book and slowly built on it. In my "plucking up" season, God began to purge things out of me that were not part of my identity. As I have discussed throughout this book, God healed me from abandonment, but this did not start until some root issues were addressed. God used my "plucking up" season to also rid me of my toxic relationships and connections. My "plucking up" season was very painful as the word denotes.

In my "time to weep" season, many tears were shed. In 2020, I lost my paternal aunt, who was a mother figure to me. Her death happened so suddenly and quickly that it knocked the wind and faith out of me. I came to a very dark and low point in my life. I questioned everything I believed in because I was certain that He would heal my aunt and save her life. When God did the exact opposite of what I expected, I spiraled down a path of feeling rejected, unloved, overlooked, undervalued, alone, and depressed. I thought there was no point of return for me after she passed. I questioned whether or not God was on my side; I felt illegitimate. I resented God and the very purpose He placed me on this earth to fulfill. With this, I spent many days soaking my pillows in tears. I cried so much that I grew tired of seeing myself cry. I couldn't hide behind the mask of strength as I had in the past; I couldn't be strong anymore. It was a season of grief as it was "a time to weep."

To everything, there is a season. I believe there is a season to love, and I am willing to wait on God to unveil love in His time.

Scripture says: Seek ye first the kingdom of God and all His righteousness and all these things will be added unto you. What does this mean? This means that God has the "things" to add to you when you seek Him. This means, don't worry about the desires of your heart, the things you want; God will manifest those things in your life when you seek Him. What does seeking God look like? Your attention is solely on God. You are an active servant for the Kingdom. You are not only focused on doing things that benefit you but also benefit others. Your time, as Paul says: Is spent on your Father's business.

There were times when I thought I was ready to build a life with someone but as much as I desired marriage, I knew I wasn't spiritually or physically mature enough to be a healthy partner. There were times I'd find myself expecting a man to fix the issues I needed to work out with God first. I really believed marriage would be the bandage to my broken heart. "If only I could be in a relationship, I would be able to ignore and avoid all the issues that arose in life," I thought. I knew if I'd been married a few years ago, I'd put too many unrealistic expectations on my spouse to fix things only God could. Don't rush into marriage expecting that it will put a band-aid on the stuff you don't want to tackle now. Marriage is neither a band-aid nor heart surgery.

Another person can never fix or heal you from the mess that you've repressed, only you and God can. Embrace where you are, don't get comfortable, and allow God to develop you. Do what you can and let God uncover and do the rest. Don't think that you need to fix yourself in order for God to bring you a spouse, leave the *fixing* to God. Allowing God into your heart gives Him access to mend the brokenness and heal your loneliness. God desires for you to become a good friend, daughter, sister, mother, and aunt, not just a prepared wife!

REFLECTION

I understand that it seems hard to believe Him for something while watching others get the very thing you've prayed for. Do you know what it feels like to be abstinent for 10 years while still waiting on the manifestation of a promise from God?

There was a time when God told me to start praying with married women for restoration in their marriage; the experience was humbling, but I gained the wisdom I needed for my future. Countless times, I've cried out to God asking, "when is it going to be my time, when are you going to do it for me, God?" Don't let what you see distract you from what God said.

God encouraged me to endure like a good servant, which means to continue to serve the Lord and He will give me my heart's desires and make good on His promise. It's hard to believe God when you don't have the evidence of what you've been praying for; so you must focus on what God says about it.

Here is what we have evidence of:

- God is faithful to His word. Isaiah 11:55
- He is not a man that He should lie. Numbers 23:19
- (Wo)Man devises plans in his heart but God orchestrates their footsteps. Proverbs 16:9
- He is a promise-keeping God. 2 Peter 3:9
- His word is true. 2 Samuel 7:28

- Every vision that He has given you for your life, will come to pass. Habakkuk 2:2
- God does not operate on our time; He operates outside of time. 2 Peter 3:8
- He has good thoughts for you and the life He has for you. His plans are to bless you. Jeremiah 29:11

Search me, O God, and know my heart: try me, and know my thoughts. (Psalm 139:23 NIV)

Wait on God

Who God has for you is better than any mate you handpicked yourself, wait on God's best. **Be still and know that He is God.**

The best thing you can do for yourself is to wait for God's best for you. There will be many imitators that will come into your life whose mission is to derail you and detour you from the promises of God. Trust me, I know that waiting is not the easiest thing but it's the best thing. Who God has for you is better than any mate you handpicked yourself, wait on God's best. God created you, so He knows what is best for you more than you know what's best for you so wait on God. In the wait, work on you.

There is a greater purpose for you than the title of wife and a wife season is not the greatest season.

LET'S PRAY

God, your word says that you give us the desires of our hearts. I trust your word to be true. I stand on your word and your promise. Lord, help me to seek your heart and things of God. Help my desires to line up with your will for my life. I know that you give us free will and I am thankful for that, but I desire to have what you will for me. I know that your plans for my life are perfect, so I give you the okay to search me. Search my heart Lord and separate my will from yours. Make me aware of my desires and cause them to line up with the word of God.

About the Author

Sade Solomon is a woman who decided to put the phrase "leap of faith" into action by betting on her dreams and shifting her career from social work to fashion. Her new focus was to relentlessly pursue the complex journey of discovering her life's true purpose and helping other women to do the same.

After earning her bachelor's degree in Human Development and Family Studies in 2009 and her associate's degree in Fashion Design in 2013, Sade launched her fashion-focused platform as a faith-based content creator in NYC in 2013. It was then that she noticed a lack of transparency and conversations within the church walls surrounding real-life topics and experiences like sex, dating, relationships, and abstinence. This led her to foster an online community where she boldly and fashionably ignites authentic, candid conversations on topics others are too timid to touch.

Sade openly shares her life-changing commitment to sexual abstinence, a journey she embarked on in 2013, on various online platforms while enlightening and inspiring many through her journey. She passionately believes that every person, despite their relationship status or sexual experience, can be equipped with the no-fluff wisdom and advice surrounding these topics.

Sade fervently believes that these topics should be discussed without shame, fear, or guilt. She is here to shift the narrative and impact lives.

www.ingramcontent.com/pod-product-compliance
Lightning Source LLC
Chambersburg PA
CBHW020436130626
46549CB00001B/170